understanding history 3

JOHN CHILD   TIM HODGE   DAVID TAYLOR

SERIES EDITOR: JOHN CHILD

HEINEMANN
EDUCATIONAL

Contents

1.1 Europe in 1914

In 1914 Europe's main **powers** (strongest countries) were rivals for land and trade and very suspicious of each other. No power wanted to be left isolated against the others, so they made **alliances** to defend themselves against attack. By 1914 Germany, Austria-Hungary and Italy had formed the **Triple Alliance**. Britain, France and Russia had formed the **Triple Entente**.

Germany feared attack from France. In 1871 Germany had defeated France in a war and taken the French provinces of **Alsace** and **Lorraine**. France wanted to take these lands back.

Other countries feared Germany. The German economy was growing rapidly. But Germany was hemmed in by the other European countries and had a small empire compared with Britain and France. It wanted to extend its **empire** to provide raw materials and a market for its growing industries.

In 1911 there was unrest in **Morocco**. This was an area of northern Africa under French control. Germany sent a battleship, *Panther*, to the Moroccan port of Agadir, saying it was coming to the defence of the Moroccans. This was an attempt to increase German influence in Africa. France and Britain had to combine to warn Germany not to interfere.

Production of new Dreadnought battleships in Britain and Germany		
Year	Britain	Germany
1906	1	–
1907	3	–
1908	2	4
1909	2	3
1910	3	1
1911	5	3
1912	3	2
1913	7	3

Britain kept its lead in the naval arms race, but it had a large coastline and a huge empire to protect. The growth of Germany's navy was seen as an act of aggression.

The sultan of Turkey leaving the Balkans, as the other powers look on. This German cartoon was drawn before the death of Queen Victoria in 1901.

Source A

A porcupine wearing a German helmet attacks the people of Alsace-Lorraine in a German cartoon drawn in 1913 after unrest there.

Source B

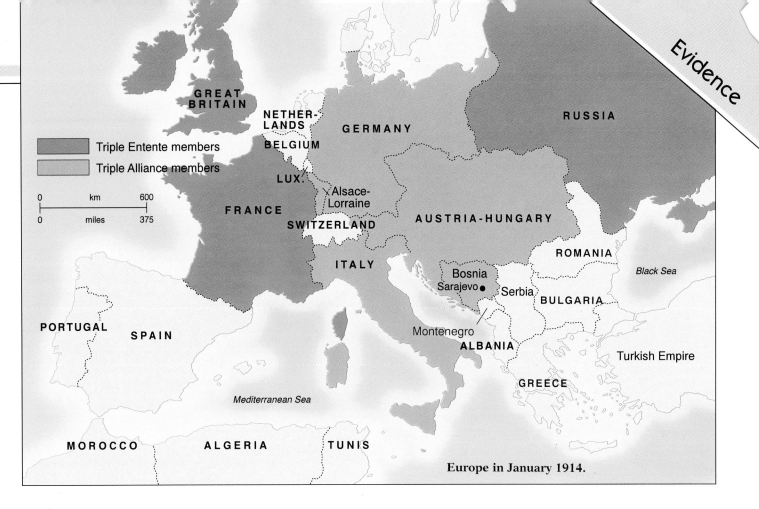

Triple Entente members
Triple Alliance members

GREAT BRITAIN
NETHER-LANDS
GERMANY
RUSSIA
BELGIUM
LUX.
Alsace-Lorraine
FRANCE
SWITZERLAND
AUSTRIA-HUNGARY
ITALY
ROMANIA
Bosnia
Sarajevo
Serbia
Black Sea
BULGARIA
PORTUGAL
SPAIN
Montenegro
ALBANIA
Turkish Empire
GREECE
Mediterranean Sea
MOROCCO
ALGERIA
TUNIS

0 km 600
0 miles 375

Europe in January 1914.

Germany was also building a **bigger navy**. Britain saw this as a threat to its own defence, trade and empire. In 1906 Britain produced its first **Dreadnought**, a powerful new battleship. Germany followed with improved ships of its own, and a **naval arms race** began.

The Balkans

The biggest rivalry between the great powers was in the **Balkans**. This was an area of south-eastern Europe which had been part of the Turkish Ottoman Empire. But Turkey had become too weak to keep control of the Balkans. In 1912 war broke out there, and Serbia, Bulgaria, Greece, Romania and Turkey fought over the land.

Some people who lived in the Balkans, such as the Serbians, wanted to unite all of the Slav people around the Black Sea into a huge new nation state. But Austria-Hungary contained many Slavs. A Slav state would break up the Austrian Empire.

Anyway, Austria wanted more land in the Balkans. In 1908, it had seized Bosnia and Herzegovina. Russia opposed Austria expansion because it would cut Russia off from the Mediterranean. Germany encouraged her ally Austria to expand because it would give Germany a direct trade route to the Mediterranean.

The tensions in the Balkans made trouble likely there. The involvement of the great powers made this dangerous for the whole of Europe.

Questions

Section A

1 Draw a diagram to show the two main alliances in Europe in 1914.

2 Describe the **tensions** (sources of possible trouble) between the alliances using the following headings:
   a tensions in Europe and the colonies.
   b tension in the Balkans.

3 Look at the table. Compare the number of British and German battleships in 1907 and 1912. What conclusions might the British government draw from these figures?

Section B

4 What impression does Source B give of Turkey?

5 How useful is Source B in telling us about the attitude of the other European powers towards Turkey?

6 a What does Source A tell us about the German government of Alsace-Lorraine?
   b Source A was first produced in a German magazine. Does this make it more or less reliable?

5

1.2 Assassination at Sarajevo

Archduke Franz Ferdinand's torn and bloodstained uniform. How far does the uniform fit the evidence of Source B?

The event which sparked off the First World War was the murder of the heir to the throne of Austria-Hungary – **Archduke Franz Ferdinand**. On Sunday 28 June 1914 he was visiting **Sarajevo** in Bosnia, which had been part of the Austrian Empire since 1908. His killers were Bosnian students from a group called the **Black Hand**. They wanted to free all Slav people from Austro-Hungarian rule. They lived in Serbia and had had military training from Serbian nationalists there. When the Archduke's visit was announced, they plotted to kill him. One of the plotters, **Gavrilo Princip**, shot the Archduke and his wife Sophie as they drove through the streets of Sarajevo in their open-topped car.

Austria-Hungary felt that it could not let the murder go unpunished. It seemed a perfect chance to attack Serbia. This would show the strength of the Hapsburg family who ruled Austria-Hungary and it would weaken the Slav nationalists who wanted to break up the Austrian Empire. It could also gain land in the Balkans for Austria-Hungary. The Austrian Foreign Minister, **Berchtold**, recommended war.

Austria-Hungary was too weak to act alone because Russia might protect Serbia. If this happened, Austria would need Germany's help. So Germany had to be consulted. On 6 July, Germany encouraged Austria to go ahead. This was the key decision on the road to war.

Nobody could prove any links between the Serbian government and the Black Hand. Despite this, on 23 July 1914 Austria sent a protest to Serbia, making ten demands. All the demands were humiliating to Serbia, but on 25 July Serbia accepted all but one. Not satisfied, Austria sent troops to the Serbian border. The tension grew. Russia announced its support for Serbia. The British Foreign Secretary, **Lord Grey**, asked for an international conference to sort out the crisis. Ignoring all this, and supported by Germany, Austria-Hungary attacked Serbia on 28 July.

One of the plotters, Cabrinovic, asked a policeman standing nearby to tell him which car the Archduke was in. The excited detective pointed in the right direction, and a few seconds later the would-be assassin knocked the cap off a hand grenade and threw it at the Archduke's car. The bomb bounced off the car but wounded 20 people, among them three of the imperial party.

Ignoring the attempt to kill him, the Archduke continued his drive through the streets of Sarajevo. Only one route-change was made, so that he could visit one of the wounded officers – but nobody told the drivers of the cars. The Archduke's car was about to follow the first two cars when the Governor of Bosnia shouted, 'What is this? Stop! You are going the wrong way!'

Stepping hard on the brake, the driver stopped the car. By chance, Gavrilo Princip, the chief plotter and the best sharp-shooter among them, was there. He took out his revolver. A policeman saw the danger and was about to grab his hand, when he was struck by a friend of the killer. Princip was only a few steps from the target. The Duchess was hit first, by a bullet aimed at the governor which penetrated the side of the car and entered her right side. The Archduke was hit seconds later. A bullet pierced the right side of his coat collar and went through the jugular vein, causing heavy bleeding; it came to a stop in the spine.

By 11.30 a.m. the imperial couple lay dead in the Governor's residence. The doctors had failed to save their lives.

From A. J. P. Taylor (editor-in-chief), 'History of the 20th Century', 1967.

Source C

This is not the crime of a single fanatic. This assassination represents Serbia's declaration of war on Austria-Hungary. If we miss this occasion, the monarchy will be exposed to new explosions of Slav, Czech, Russian and Italian ambitions. Austria-Hungary must wage war for political reasons.

General von Hotzendorf, Austro-Hungarian chief of staff, speaking immediately after the assassination in 1914.

Source D

A French cartoon, dated 1908, showing the expansion of Austria-Hungary in the Balkans. The Emperor of Austria-Hungary and Prince Ferdinand of Bulgaria are tearing apart the Turkish Empire.

World War

Within a week, the alliance systems of the great powers turned this local war into a world war. On 30 July, Russia mobilized its armies to protect Serbia. Germany declared war on Russia on 1 August, and invaded France two days later.

There is a simple reason why events moved so fast. Germany's big fear was having to fight Russia in the east and Russia's ally, France, in the west at the same time. But it would take several weeks for the huge Russian war machine to get its troops organized. Germany had a special plan.

The German plan, called the **Schlieffen Plan** after the general who invented it, started with a huge and rapid attack on France. If the Germans could defeat France in six weeks, they could then turn all their forces upon Russia. This plan depended on an attack through Belgium, because France's defences were too strong along its border with Germany. As soon as the Russian troops started to mobilize, therefore, Germany had to attack France. Any delay might ruin Germany's chances.

Britain did not want to go to war to defend Serbia. But it could not stand by and watch Germany defeat France and Russia. If Germany dominated the whole of mainland Europe, Britain would never be safe. Britain had also guaranteed Belgian safety from attack in a treaty signed in 1839 – and the Belgian coast would be an ideal place from which to launch an enemy invasion of Britain. Britain demanded that Germany withdraw its troops by midnight on 4 August. There was no withdrawal, and Britain declared war on Germany.

Questions

Section A

1 a Why did Austria-Hungary declare war on Serbia?
  b Why did Russia want to defend Serbia?
  c Why did Germany help Austria-Hungary against Russia?
  d Why did Germany attack France?
  e Why did Britain declare war on Germany?

Section B

2 'The story of the murder of Archduke Franz Ferdinand shows that sometimes events in history rely upon chance.' Do you agree?

3 The following list gives some possible causes of the First World War:
  ● tension between the great powers
  ● Slav nationalists wanted freedom from Austria
  ● murder of Franz Ferdinand
  ● Austria-Hungary was bullying Serbia
  ● Germany was encouraging the Austrians
  ● the Schlieffen Plan
  ● Britain's guarantee to Belgium.

Explain how all these causes are connected.

1.3 Who Was To Blame?

The causes of the First World War were complicated. Historians have suggested different interpretations about who was to blame. In this unit, Sources A, G and H are extracts from the work of three historians who have very different opinions about who was to blame.

Source A

On 6 July, Bethmann, the German Foreign Minister, told the Austrians, 'Austria must judge what is to be done with Serbia. but whatever Austria's decision, you can count upon it that Germany will stand by you as an ally.' He added, 'If war must break out, better now than in one or two years' time when the Triple Entente will be stronger.'

Kaiser Wilhelm and Bethmann did more than give Austria-Hungary a free hand. They encouraged the Austrians to start a war and to risk the consequences. If it came to world war, they were confident of winning now but less confident of winning later. If they had wanted a peaceful solution, they would have approached the British at once. Instead, they did nothing, hoping to keep Britain neutral in a continental war.

From A. J. P. Taylor, 'The Struggle for Mastery in Europe', 1954.

Source B

A British postcard from 1914 showing Kaiser Wilhelm.

Source C

A German cigarette card from about 1900, with a quotation from a famous German general, Moltke, who said, 'War is an element in God's natural order of things.'

Source D

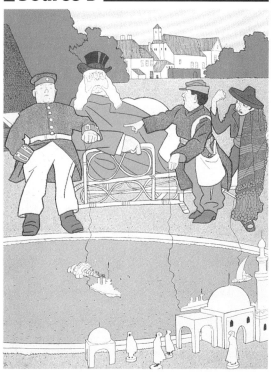

A cartoon drawn during the Moroccan crisis of 1911 (see Unit 1.1). The French and Spanish children playing round the pond turn to Uncle John Bull (Britain), who looks sternly on at the German boy who is interrupting their game. Britain's strong stand in support of France over Morocco forced Germany to withdraw its demands.

Source E

A German cartoon from about 1910. Germany is shown peacefully watering his garden. An uncivilized bully, his Russian neighbour, threatens him from over the fence.

Source F

A cartoon dated about 1900. It shows Germany breast-feeding the Prussian army and kicking away the thinker. The cartoonist believed that Germany gave too much influence to generals and that this made it a warlike state.

Source G

The Kaiser's aims were largely defensive. He had to prop up his ally, Austria. The longer Austria's decline went on, the weaker the Triple Alliance became. He needed to break free of the encircling powers of the Triple Entente; he needed to fend off Russia, the military revenge by France and trading domination by Britain. He dreaded war on two fronts. He felt that war was bound to happen so he had to decide the timing. He had to create a mighty army and navy and give power to their leaders.

From Ed Rayner and Ron Stapley, 'GCSE World History', 1988.

Source H

Lord Grey could have prevented war. Early in the crisis he could have responded to France and Russia and given a strong warning to Germany that Britain would take the side of the Franco–Russian Alliance. This would have led Germany to try to hold back the Austrians. It might have prevented the declaration of war on Serbia. Or Lord Grey could have warned France and Russia that Britain would remain neutral. Russia would then have hesitated with its mobilization against Austria and Germany.

From Sidney Bradshaw Fay, 'Origins of the World War', 1930.

Questions

Section A

1 For anyone studying the causes of the First World War, Sources B–F are **primary sources** and Sources A, G and H are **secondary sources**. Explain why.

2 Look at the primary sources.
 a Which shows Germany as aggressive and militaristic?
 b Which shows Germany as peaceful, even frightened?

3 What does Source D say about Britain's role in European affairs before the First World War?

Section B

4 Read Sources A, G and H. Each has a different interpretation about who was to blame for the war. Make a table like the one below and fill it in to explain what each source says about who was to blame and which primary sources support each interpretation.

Source	Who was to blame for the war?	Which sources support this interpretation?
A G H		

5 'Interpretations depend upon the selection of sources.' Having answered question **4**, what do you think about this statement?

2.1 The War Begins

The **First World War** began in August 1914. Everyone expected it to be over by Christmas. But it proved to be a very different war from the one expected. On the one side were the **Central Powers**: Germany, Austria-Hungary, Bulgaria and Turkey. On the other were the **Allies**: France, Russia, Serbia, Belgium and Britain. Italy joined the Allies in 1915.

On 3 August the German chief of staff, **von Moltke**, put the Schlieffen Plan into operation. Some of the German troops defended the border with France near **Metz** and a few looked after the Russian border in the east. But the main German force invaded France through **Belgium**. The plan was to encircle **Paris** and then attack the main French forces from the rear. After quickly defeating France, the German army could then travel east to face the slow-moving Russian forces. But almost immediately things went wrong.

Source A

No experience had led me to expect a defensive war of positions. All my thoughts were concentrated upon a war of speedy movement.

General Sir John French, looking back on the events of 1914.

Source B

They came on until, as we shot them, the fallen were heaped in an awful barricade. But those amazing Germans kept creeping closer. Our machine guns inflicted terrible carnage on them.

A Belgian officer describing the German advance in 1914.

Source C

That men who have retreated for ten days, half dead with fatigue, should be able to take up their rifles and attack when the bugle sounds, is a thing upon which we never counted.

A German general, von Kluck, describing the French army in 1914.

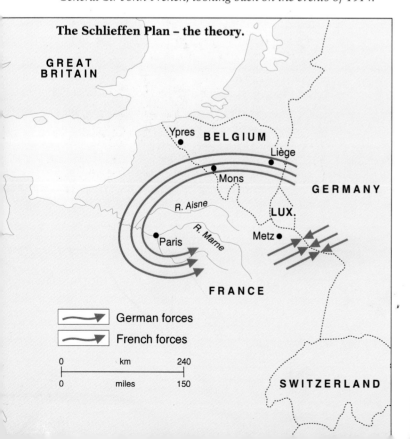

The Schlieffen Plan – the theory.

German forces
French forces

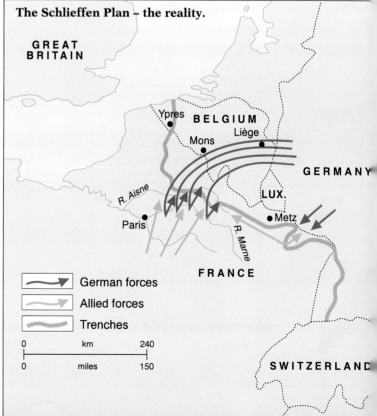

The Schlieffen Plan – the reality.

German forces
Allied forces
Trenches

Source D

THE GERMANS MAKE SAUSAGES AND WE'LL SKIN 'EM

A British postcard from 1914.

The Schlieffen Plan fails

First, the Germans met tough resistance in Belgium. They were delayed for ten days at **Liège**. Then the **British Expeditionary Force (BEF)**, 125,000 well-trained men led by General French, held them up at **Mons**. On 19 August the Russian army attacked, before the German armies had reached Paris. Germany had to withdraw troops to protect its eastern frontier. New methods of transport, such as steamships, railways and lorries moved defensive troops into position faster than expected, and this weakened the Schlieffen Plan further. The French commander-in-chief, **General Joffre**, used almost 5000 trains in troop movements.

Despite all this, by 4 September the exhausted German troops had reached the **River Marne**, almost in sight of Paris. French troops from Metz had failed to take Alsace and Lorraine and retreated to help defend Paris. The BEF joined them. In addition, reserve troops were sent from Paris to help. At one time, 250 taxis were used to send in fresh troops. The **Battle of the Marne** lasted a week and involved 2 million men. Finally, the Germans were forced back. They retreated 60 kilometres to the **River Aisne**, where they dug trenches defended by machine-gun posts.

The Allies could not break through these defences. They dug parallel trenches. Each side extended their trenches so that the enemy could not get behind them. Fierce battles were fought to gain as much land as possible before the trenches were dug. At the **First Battle of Ypres** one British division lost 10,774 of its 12,000 men. By the end of 1914 the trenches stretched from Switzerland in the south to the English Channel in the north. It was **stalemate**.

Questions

Section A

1 Draw a timeline, showing the years 1914–18. Mark your timeline with the key events of 1914 discussed in this unit. (Questions in later units will ask you to add the key events of the rest of the war.)

2 Everybody in Europe thought that their side would win the war; they all thought it would not last long. How does Source D get this optimism across?

Section B

3 Why did the British and French hopes of a quick victory fail?

4 'The German hopes of a quick victory failed because of French bravery.' Do you agree?

2.2 Trench Warfare on the Western Front

A German cartoon from 1916 commenting on the tactics of the military leaders. The Crown Prince tells his father, the Kaiser, 'We must have a higher pile if we are ever to see Verdun.' Verdun was a French stronghold.

The trenches across Belgium and France became known as the **Western Front**. Each side constantly attacked. Thousands of men were sent '**over the top**'. This meant climbing out of the trenches and charging the enemy lines. The defenders protected themselves with barbed wire and machine guns. They also had aeroplanes which could be used to monitor the build-up of troops before an attack. Extra troops could be rushed to the threatened area by using lorries and railways. Heavy shelling churned up the land between the trenches and made it difficult to cross. It was so difficult to capture that it became known as **no man's land**.

Puzzled by the failure of massed attacks, the only solution the generals could think of was to make the attacks even larger. The result was appalling casualties. The German generals even tried to send clouds of poisonous gas over Allied trenches, but these failed. The weapons of defence were stronger than the weapons of attack. Neither side could break the stalemate. Victories were measured in yards not miles. Success was losing fewer men than the enemy. Each side tried to wear down the other in a **war of attrition**.

Source C

We occupy a crater and get surrounded. Two fellows with a flame-thrower move towards us. One carries the tin of petrol on his back, the other has the hose from which the fire spouts. If they get near enough to use it, we are done for, since we cannot retreat across the open ground.

We open fire on them, but they work nearer; things look bad. Bentinck is lying in the hole with us. When he sees that we cannot escape, he takes a rifle, crawls out of the crater and, lying down propped on his elbows, he takes aim. He fires – the same moment a bullet smacks into him. Still he lies there and aims again; at last he fires, lets the gun drop and slips back into the hole. One of the flamethrowers is hit, he falls, the hose slips, squirting fire on all sides and he burns.

Bentinck has a chest wound. After a while a shell fragment hits him and smashes away his chin. The same fragment carries on to tear open Leer's hip. He bleeds quickly. Like an empty tube; after a couple of minutes he collapses.

From 'All Quiet on the Western Front', 1929. This novel was written by Erich Remarque, who was a German soldier in the First World War.

Source D

Until that time [1917], both sides conducted their battles on similar lines. Artillery blazed away at the enemy's wire and trenches for weeks on end. Then, over the heavy, mutilated ground, we stumbled into attack. Usually we ran up against large patches of uncut wire. Many men were often mown down by machine gun fire. The element of surprise was always missing. In order to collect the huge mass of guns and shells needed, railway lines were built to the back of the lines. Enemy aeroplanes and spies soon knew what was going on.

Even if we overcame these obstacles, we could not possibly advance farther than 4000 yards or so. We carried packs with three days' rations and entrenching tools, 180 rounds of ammunition and grenades. A Mills bomb weighed about 5 lb [2.2 kg] and the cartridges quite a bit. Burdened like pack horses, we were expected to fight for our lives with the bayonet if the occasion arose.

You always knew when a man was shot dead. A wounded man always tried to break his fall. A dead man generally fell forward, buckling from the knees, waist, neck and ankles simultaneously.

Captain A. O. Pollard, VC, describing what it was like to go 'over the top'.

Source E

The attack by Reserve Army today was very successful. All objectives were gained on a front 300 to 500 yards in depth. A total of 1018 prisoners have passed through the cages. Our losses were under 1600. Mr Balfour visited the battlefield today and greatly enjoyed himself.

Extract dated October 1916 from the diary of Earl Haig, the commander-in-chief of the British forces. Balfour was a British polititian.

A scene across no man's land from a painting called 'The Harvest of Battle', by C. R. W. Nevinson, 1921.

Life in the trenches

The armies were in the trenches until 1918. For the soldiers in the trenches, life was harsh, squalid and boring; there were long periods with nothing to do. There was always the risk of enemy snipers and artillery fire, or occasional gas or aeroplane attacks. But the real danger came with the order to go 'over the top'.

The front line trenches were about two metres deep. The bottom was lined with wooden duck-boards to prevent people from sinking into the mud. The trench tops were lined with sandbags. Soldiers slept in shelters dug out of the walls of the trenches. These were baking hot in summer and freezing cold in winter. Junior officers, like captains and majors, who led companies of about 250 men, lived with their men. Senior staff officers worked from headquarters well behind the lines.

Soldiers did not spend all of their time on the front line. In an average month, each soldier would spend two weeks on active service and two weeks resting behind the lines. On active service, some of the time would be spent in the front line of trenches, confronting the enemy. The rest of the time was spent in the support trenches behind the front line. Thousands of communication trenches linked the support trenches to the front line.

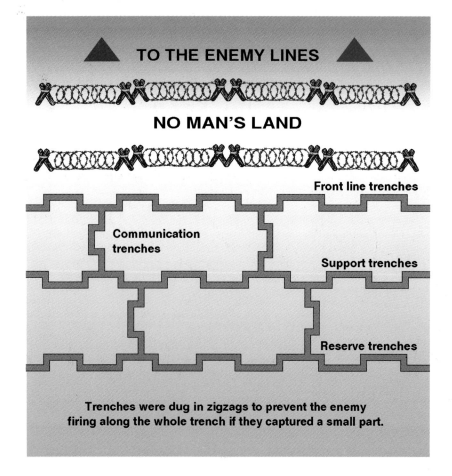

Trenches were dug in zigzags to prevent the enemy
firing along the whole trench if they captured a small part.

The trench system.

Source F

Army food was monotonous. Tinned bully beef was the usual. We were always hungry. Many times we only got one slice of bread, often without butter or jam, for breakfast and hard biscuits for tea. These were so hard that you had to put them on a firm surface and smash them with a stone or something. Sometimes when drinking water did not arrive, we had to boil rainwater from shell holes.

A British soldier who served on the front line in 1915.

Source G

To add to the general discomfort, the trenches were alive with rats. The knowledge that the gigantic trench rats had grown fat through feeding on the dead bodies in no man's land made the soldiers hate them more fiercely than almost anything else.

From S. Case, 'The First World War', 1976.

Source H

One of my stretcher bearers has a foot swollen to three times its normal size; a great helpless bright pink lump. He has been working in the mud for all of four days. I shall be surprised if he doesn't lose that foot.

Sergeant E. W. Simon, writing from the Somme in 1916. The wet conditions caused an infection known as trenchfoot. It affected thousands of troops.

Source I

One is overcome by a peculiar sour, heavy and penetrating smell of corpses. Rising over a plank bridge, you find that its middle is supported only by the body of a long-dead horse. Men that were killed last October lie half in swamp. The legs of an Englishman stick out into a trench, the corpse being built into the parapet; a soldier hangs his rifle on them. A little brook runs through the trench, and everyone uses the water for drinking and washing; it is the only water they have. Nobody minds the Englishman, who is rotting away a few steps farther up. At one point, I saw 22 dead horses, still harnessed together. Cattle and pigs lie about, half rotten, broken trees, crater upon crater in the roads and fields. Such is a six months old battlefield.

From Rudolf Binding, 'Fatalist at War'. Binding was a German soldier.

Source J

From a painting showing Canadian troops at the Battle of Ypres, which began in July 1917.

Source K

Royal Army Medical Corps removing the injured after the capture of an enemy trench at the Battle of Messines Ridge in 1917.

Questions

Section A

1 Read Sources C and D. Make a list of the things that soldiers might have taken with them when they went 'over the top'.

2 Look at Sources A and E. What do they tell us about the military leaders in the First World War?

3 Read Sources F–I. Judging by these, which of the pictures in this unit gives the best impression of life in the trenches? Give reasons for your answer.

Section B

4 The war on the Western Front was unlike any previous European war. Three special features of this war were:
 ● new weapons
 ● the stalemate
 ● horrific living conditions in the trenches.
 Write a paragraph on each of these features describing them in detail.

5 Are the three features you have described in question **4** all separate, or are they connected in any way?

2.3 The Great Battles of 1915–17

1915–16

In January 1915 the French launched an attack on the German trenches at **Champagne**; they won 500 metres of land and lost 50,000 men. The British attack at **Neuve Chapelle** in March was no more successful. It lasted two months, gained only a tiny area of land and cost 11,000 lives.

In April 1915 the **Second Battle of Ypres** took place. This was a German offensive which started with a **gas attack**. Clouds of chlorine killed two whole brigades of Frenchmen, almost 10,000 soldiers, before the German breakthrough was halted.

In September 1915, 100,000 British soldiers went 'over the top' at **Loos**. By the end of the month 60,000 of them were dead. Overall in 1915 the Allies captured a total of 10 square kilometres of land along the Western Front and lost almost 400,000 men.

Attacks subsided during the winter of 1915–16. But in February 1916 the German **General Falkenhayn** launched a huge attack on the city of **Verdun**, which was protected by thirteen concrete forts. The German artillery fired 23 million shells, killing 315,000 on the French side. But **General Philippe Pétain** had been ordered to save the city. He told his men, 'They shall not pass.' After five months and losses of 280,000 men, the Germans gave up the attack.

_ Source B

Kitchener seemed to me very ignorant of what is being done and how trenches are being attacked and bombarded. He admitted that the nature of the modern lines of defence was new to him and he felt 'quite at sea with the subject'.

General Haig reporting a conversation with Lord Kitchener, 1915.

_ Source C

Just behind the French lines there are towns which the French must defend to the last man. If they do, then the French army will be exhausted by its bloody losses; if it lets them go, the damage to French morale will be enormous.

General Falkenhayn explaining his attack on Verdun in 1916.

_ Source D

Who told them that artillery fire would pound the barbed wire to pieces? Any Tommy could have told them that shell fire lifts wire up and drops it down in a worse tangle than before.

George Coppard, who fought at the Battle of the Somme in 1916, in his memoirs, 'With a Machine Gun to Cambrai'. A 'Tommy' is an ordinary private soldier.

_ Source A

The Second Battle of Ypres, painted by W. B. Wollen. Canadian troops are shown beating off a German attack. Five thousand Canadians were lost in this battle, but the artist shows the fighting as glorious rather than horrifying.

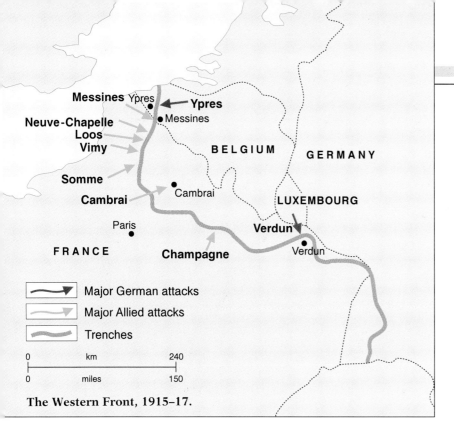

The Western Front, 1915–17.

While this German offensive was still going on, in July 1916 the British launched their biggest attack yet along the River Somme. They began with a seven-day artillery bombardment, firing a million shells into the German trenches. Over 200,000 soldiers were sent into the **Battle of the Somme** on the first day, and 20,000 died. The story was repeated almost every day for over three months. The British gained about 15 kilometres and lost 620,000 men; the Germans lost 450,000.

1917

In early 1917 the new French commander, **General Nivelle**, started another attack at **Champagne**. Losses were so high that thousands of French soldiers deserted and there was a massive mutiny. Only ruthless punishments restored discipline in the French army.

The British had more success. For months, engineers had been digging nineteen tunnels under no man's land and into a hill occupied by the Germans at **Messines**. They packed the tunnels with 500,000 kg of TNT explosive. On 7 June the hill was blown up. Windows shook as far away as London. The hill disappeared, and the British advanced several kilometres.

But two British failures followed. First, in August 1917 Field Marshal Haig ordered the **Third Battle of Ypres** (also known as the **Battle of Passchendaele**). The attack started with a bombardment of almost 5 million shells, but in the next three months the British won only 800 metres of mud at a cost of 300,000 men. Then, in November it looked as if British tanks had made a breakthrough at **Cambrai**. But the infantry could not control the land gained, and the Germans recaptured it all.

Source E

> It was a deadly mixture: the patriotism and respect for authority of the working-class infantry and the optimism, bordering on belief in infallibility, of the upper-class officers who increasingly put their faith in bigger and bigger attacks.

From Wolfgang Steglich, 'History of the 20th Century', 1967.

Source F

> It seemed as if the whole French army was gathered there for the victorious assault. The air was filled with enthusiasm, and a heroic mood prevailed. Officers and soldiers refused to go on leave so as not to miss the great offensive. The men were already drunk with victory.

A French soldier recalling General Nivelle's offensive at Champagne in 1917.

Questions

Section A

1 a Mark on your timeline of the war the key events on the Western Front, 1915–17.
  b Make a table showing the key attacks. Use the following headings:
  ● date
  ● battle
  ● attacking force
  ● casualties
  ● result of attack.

2 Were there any changes in the military tactics used on the Western Front between 1915 and 1917?

Section B

3 Look at Sources B,C and D. The tactics used by the generals on the Western Front didn't work. But they continued to believe in them. Why was this?

4 Look at Sources E and F. The tactics used by the generals on the Western Front didn't work. Why did the soldiers continue to trust them?

2.4 The Other Fronts

Fighting was not restricted to the Western Front. The **land war** was fought in other parts of Europe and even in other continents.

The Eastern Front

The **Russian army** mobilized much faster than Germany had hoped. However, the experienced German generals **Hindenburg** and **Ludendorff** were sent to the Eastern Front; by mid-September 1914 they had won victories at the **Battle of Tannenberg** and the **Battle of the Masurian Lakes**.

Russia had a huge army of over 7 million men, but they were poorly equipped. They had only 4 million rifles; many soldiers had to take weapons from the dead. The Russians lost 250,000 men within a month. They were also driven back by Austria-Hungary.

By 1915 Russian armies had been forced over 300 kilometres back into their own country. They had a brief period of success

Source A

This land does not only hold Russians and lice. Flies and fleas also wage war here. Of the flies one cannot really speak or they fly into one's mouth. The fleas are a bit more cheerful. Every respectable person has at least six in his shirt. They are as big as young beetles. I get a bag of about twelve every morning. The captain always beats me and puts me to shame with the size of his bag, but then he gets up a half an hour later.

From the diary of a German soldier in Galicia, on the Eastern Front, dated 10 September 1916.

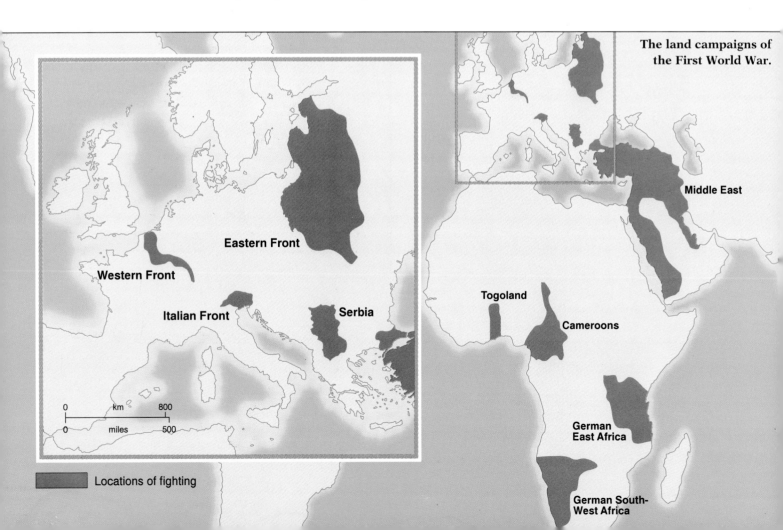

The land campaigns of the First World War.

Eastern Front

Western Front

Italian Front

Serbia

Middle East

Togoland

Cameroons

German East Africa

German South-West Africa

km 0 — 800
miles 0 — 500

Locations of fighting

Source B

'The Last Day of Resistance of Belgrade', painted by Oscar Laske, 1915.

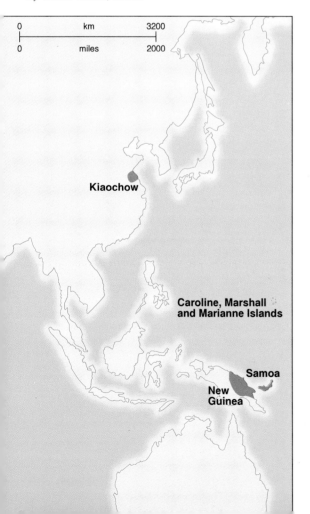

under **General Brusilov** in 1916, but after that they were forced to dig trenches and defend. Conditions were much like those on the Western Front – but colder.

Meanwhile **Serbia** was being crushed. After holding out for some months against the Austrians, the Serbs found themselves attacked by German and Bulgarian troops. They fought hand-to-hand battles in the streets of the capital, **Belgrade**. But by the end of 1915, Serbia had fallen.

Italy joined the war on the Eastern Front in May 1915. The Allies had promised Italy land in exchange for its support. The Italian attack on Austria-Hungary across icy mountains to the **River Isonzo** soon ground to a halt.

For the Allies, 1917 was a terrible year on the Eastern Front. The first blow came in Russia. The people there were suffering such hardships and the war was going so badly that the Russian ruler, Tsar Nicholas, was overthrown (see Unit 2.7). In October 1917, a Communist government came to power. It was led by **Vladimir Lenin**. The Communists disagreed with the war against Germany. Within days, Russia withdrew from the war.

Worse was to come. Also in October, German forces joined Austrians to defeat the Italians at the **Battle of Caporetto**. Thousands of soldiers turned and ran. The Italian generals ordered a retreat of 100 kilometres to the **River Piave**.

Africa and the Far East

Germany had four colonies in Africa. Three of these – Togoland, the Cameroons and German South-West Africa – added together were almost the size of Europe. The Allies captured all of them by 1916. Only German East Africa remained in German hands until the end of the war.

Source C

I'm up here in German East Africa. I came up with 150 men. We have Belgian Congo Native troops with us. They are cannibals and it's great to see them 'scoffing' the Germans as we blot them out.

From a letter dated February 1916 from Private Fred Bambridge, in what is now Zimbabwe.

19

In the **Far East, ANZAC** troops (Australian and New Zealand Army Corps) captured the German colonies of Samoa and New Guinea in 1914. In the same year Japan captured the German trading base at Kiaochow in China, and the German Marshall Islands, Caroline Islands and Marianne Islands in the Pacific.

The Gallipoli Campaign

By early 1915 there was stalemate on the Western and Eastern Fronts. **Winston Churchill**, Britain's First Lord of the Admiralty, came up with a plan to break that stalemate. If the Allies could defeat **Turkey**, then they could get supplies to Russia through the Black Sea and start direct attacks from the south on Austria-Hungary and Bulgaria. He proposed an invasion of the **Gallipoli peninsula** – a strip of land which controlled the **Dardanelles**, the entrance to the Black Sea.

In April 1915 thousands of British and ANZAC troops landed on the Gallipoli beaches. But the Turkish army was waiting in very strong machine gun posts on the cliffs overlooking the shore. The landings were a disastrous failure. Even when they struggled inland, all the Allied forces could do was dig themselves into trenches. Short of water, suffering intense heat followed by severe cold and plagued with flies, they endured some of the worst conditions of the war.

The Turkish soldiers put up unexpectedly strong resistance. By the end of 1915 it was clear that Gallipoli would not be taken. All the Allied soldiers were evacuated. The invasion had gained no land, at the cost of 200,000 lives.

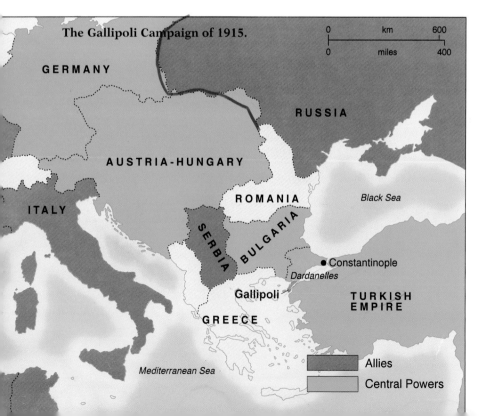

The Gallipoli Campaign of 1915.

GERMANY

RUSSIA

AUSTRIA-HUNGARY

ROMANIA

Black Sea

ITALY

SERBIA

BULGARIA

Constantinople

Dardanelles

Gallipoli

TURKISH EMPIRE

GREECE

Mediterranean Sea

Allies

Central Powers

Source D

The War Council had been sitting all day. Churchill revealed his plan for an attack on the Dardanelles. The atmosphere changed. Fatigue was forgotten. We turned eagerly from the dreary vista of a slogging match on the Western Front to movement in the Mediterranean.

The Secretary of the British War Council.

Source E

About 100 yards from the beach, the enemy opened fire. Several were hit in the boat. As soon as I felt it touch, I dashed over the side into three feet of water and rushed for the barbed wire on the beach. I got over it in a storm of lead. Only Maunsell and two others had managed to follow me. The sea was absolutely crimson with blood.

Recollections of Major Shaw, who landed at Gallipoli on 25 April 1915.

Source F

The Allied commander, Hamilton, allowed the advancing troops to settle down for breakfast. When the meal was over, large numbers of Turkish riflemen had gathered. At Suvla Bay, the commanding officer, Stopford, did not go ashore. After congratulating his men, it is claimed, he went off for his afternoon nap.

From Barry Bates, 'The First World War', 1984.

Source G

Soldiers! You must drive the enemy into the sea. He dare not come out of his trenches and attack you. You must not be afraid of his fire. You know that the greatest happiness awaits him who gives up his life for Allah in this holy war.

An order issued to the Turkish troops by their German commander, Colonel von Sodernstern, 30 April 1915.

Source H

The landing at Suvla Bay, Gallipoli. This was painted by Second Lieutenant R. C. Lewis during the action, using the dye from cigarette packets.

Source I

A terrific thunderstorm was followed by an icy hurricane; then a blizzard, heavy snow and bitter frost. Trenches were flooded. Many drowned in the trenches and more died of exposure. There were over 3000 cases of frostbite. We were entirely unprepared. There were no precautions against frostbite and no stocks of warm clothing.

Field Marshal Birdwood describing conditions at Gallipoli, 27 November 1915.

The Middle East

Most of the Middle East was controlled by Turkey, Germany's ally. But many of the Arabs in the Middle East resented Turkish rule. Britain sent several officers, including **Colonel T. E. Lawrence** (Lawrence of Arabia), into the Middle East to organize the Arabs. Lawrence spoke Arabic and understood Arab customs. He led a campaign of guerrilla warfare against the Turks, attacking Turkish outposts and blowing up their railway lines. Soon the Turks were offering a reward of £20,000 for his capture. By 1918 **General Allenby** was able to lead British forces from Egypt into Palestine against the Turkish army. He captured Jerusalem, Damascus, Beirut and Aleppo, and took 75,000 prisoners for the loss of just 5000 men. The Turks were forced to withdraw further and further. In October 1918 they accepted defeat and withdrew from the war.

Questions

Section A

1 Mark on your timeline of the First World War the main events of the land campaigns outside the Western Front.

2 Describe events:
   a on the Eastern Front.
   b in Africa.
   c in the Far East.

3 Where were the Allies most successful outside the Western Front? Explain your answer.

4 How reliable are Sources B, C and H likely to be?

Section B

5 Why did Britain decide to attack the Gallipoli peninsula?

6 Why did the Gallipoli campaign fail?

2.5 The War at Sea

In 1906 Britain built a new battleship called **HMS *Dreadnought***. The ship's armour plating was 28 cm thick on the sides and 35 cm on the decks. It travelled at 22 knots and carried 37 guns and five torpedo tubes. German sailors started to call their own ships 'five minute ships' – how long they thought they would last against a Dreadnought. Both countries raced to build more of them.

In August 1914 British ships sank three German light cruisers and one destroyer at the **Battle of Heligoland Bight**. Soon afterwards they sank the German cruiser *Blucher* at the **Battle of Dogger Bank**. In November 1914 the German **Admiral von Spee** sank a small squadron of old British ships in the Pacific, near **Coronel** in Chile. But by December that year seven British ships had hunted down von Spee's squadron off the **Falkland Islands**. They sank four of his five ships; von Spee, his sons and 2300 German sailors drowned.

Both fleets spent most of the war safe in home ports. They were afraid of submarines and mines. Britain used a few ships, submarines and mines to **blockade** German ports. This was to stop German merchant ships from importing or exporting any goods.

The Battle of Jutland

In January 1916 **Admiral von Scheer** was placed in charge of the German High Seas Fleet. He devised a plan to use a few German ships in the North Sea to lure the British fleet out to sea. He would then follow with the main fleet 80 kilometres behind to catch the British ships unaware. But the British had captured his secret codes and knew his plans.

On 31 May, the German 'bait' sailed into the North Sea. The British sent a few ships under **Admiral Beatty** to meet him. After a short skirmish, Beatty turned north.

Total losses at the Battle of Jutland		
	Britain	*Germany*
Battleships	–	1
Battle cruisers	3	1
Cruisers	3	4
Destroyers	8	5
Men	6077	1551

Source A

HMS 'Lion' in action at the Battle of Jutland, 1916.

A British government poster, 1915. The medal in the corner is labelled 'Facsimile of medal struck by Germany to commemorate the event'. The medal shows, on one side, a cartoon of Death selling tickets and on the other, the 'Lusitania' sinking.

Source B

The 'bait', with Scheer and the main German fleet following, chased him. They did not know that Beatty was luring the German ships right into the path of the British Grand Fleet, led by **Admiral Jellicoe**.

Just before 6 p.m., the two fleets – 259 ships in all, carrying 100,000 men – met in the mist off the coast of Jutland. A battle raged all through the evening. High-explosive shells proved more effective against the ships' armour than expected. The British ships seemed particularly vulnerable. There were 25 ships sunk and over 6000 men killed or drowned.

After dark, Scheer took his fleet back to port. Jellicoe, fearing German submarine attacks, decided not to chase him. The German fleet took no further part in the rest of the war.

The U-boats

The other area of naval activity was under the water. In February 1915 Germany announced that it would use its submarines, called **U-boats**, to sink any ships sailing in British waters. The Germans aimed to cut off Britain's supplies of equipment and food.

This strategy caused casualties among neutral citizens. For example, on 7 May 1915 the British liner ***Lusitania***, sailing from New York to Liverpool, was sunk. Over 1000 passengers and crew were drowned. Many of them were Americans. In the USA the public was outraged. Afraid that the USA would join the war, Germany reduced its U-boat activity in 1916.

By 1917, however, Germany was desperate to win the war. Unrestricted submarine warfare resumed. The Germans had 200 U-boats by this time and they sank one in four ships entering British waters. By April, Britain had only six weeks' food left. The Royal Navy responded by placing **mines** around German ports, using **depth charges** and employing 'Q-ships' – armed ships disguised as merchant vessels. But the tactic which saved Britain was the **convoy system**. Merchant ships sailed in groups protected by Royal Navy destroyers. Britain sank 39 U-boats in 1917 and 69 in 1918. British losses fell, and Britain avoided starvation.

Questions

Section A

1 Mark on your timeline of the war the key events of the war at sea.

2 Historians are divided about who won the Battle of Jutland. Why do you think this is?

3 Who do you think won the Battle of Jutland?

4 a What were U-boats?
  b Why were U-boats a special worry for the British?

5 How important do you think the events at sea were in the First World War? Give reasons for your answer.

Section B

6 Look at Source B.
  a What information do you think the artist had about the sinking when drawing this poster?
  b What was the purpose of the poster?

7 Do you think that Source B gives any information to historians of the First World War?

8 Do you think that Source B gives any **reliable** information to historians?

2.6 New Technology at War

The First World War was the first war between industrialized nations using the **technology of the modern world**. This changed warfare.

Transport and communications

Transport was different from that used in any previous war. About 5000 trains took the Allied troops to their defensive positions in 1914; 250 taxis took reserves to the Battle of the Marne; thousands of lorries kept Verdun supplied in 1916. Railways and motor transport had never been used like this before.

Communication by radio and telephone was also a recent development in 1914. Both technologies became vital to the troops in the trenches.

However, we must not overestimate these changes. It was still normal to use horses for haulage, and dogs and pigeons for carrying messages.

Source A

At Y Beach, 2000 men landed and sat about all day waiting. One mile round the coast, at W Beach, the landing was made at huge cost. What a waste, just because of an absence of information about what was happening on the other beaches.

Statement by an officer at Gallipoli in 1915. The attack was co-ordinated from the warships at sea, which made telephone links impossible.

Source B

Human remains, arms, legs, knapsacks, blankets, etc. hung on the trees. We watched Boches [Germans] flying as much as three or four hundred feet in the air.

A French gunner describing the effect of First World War artillery fire.

Source C

A German cartoon wondering how far mechanized warfare might go.

Source D

First World War fire power.

Weapons

Artillery also changed. Cannon had been used for centuries, but never so many of them. Before the Battle of the Somme 2000 guns fired almost 2 million shells on the enemy trenches. The British army used 170 million shells during the four years of the war. Long-distance bombardments came into use. By 1918 a German gun called Big Bertha could fire shells at Paris from 120 kilometres away.

The design of shells changed, too. High-explosive shells were used against buildings or ships, shrapnel shells with thin casings filled with lead pellets were used against men. Artillery fire killed hundreds of thousands of men. It also churned up the ground and made attacks much more difficult.

Machine guns had been used as early as the American Civil War (1861–5). But by the end of the First World War companies such as Vickers in Britain were producing new machine guns which could fire 600 bullets a minute. They had greater fire power than a whole company of 250 men with rifles.

Industry also produced another new weapon: **gas**. The Germans used chlorine to attack the Allies at Ypres in April 1915. Phosgene gas was also used, and then mustard gas, which burned the lungs and left men dying in agony. Gas was not really effective. Cumbersome gas masks were issued to all men (and many horses). However, attackers as well as defenders had to wear masks; in the end gas just slowed down the pace of advances.

Source E

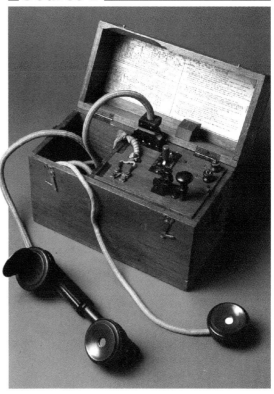

A First World War field telephone. This one is a Fullerphone which could be used as a telephone and a buzzer telegraph using Morse code. Each side tried to tap into the other's telephone lines. Secret messages were sent in code.

Source F

THE TANK
is a travelling fortress
that clears the way for
our soldiers.

It cuts through the wire–under fire
It saves lives
It is *our* War discovery
It is a matter of pride to help to
build Tanks.

A British poster of the period, appealing for money to build tanks.

Tanks were used in warfare for the first time in a British attack at the Somme in 1916. At first they could only travel at about 5 kilometres per hour. But they were a big boost to morale, and industry worked on improved designs throughout the war. By 1918 the Anglo-American Mark VIII could carry a crew of eight men into battle firing 208 shells and up to 13,000 bullets.

Tanks sometimes caused significant breakthroughs, like the one at Cambrai in 1917. But they remained very unreliable throughout the war. Of the 525 tanks used at the Battle of Amiens in 1918, only 25 were still in working order after four days.

By 1918 Rolls Royce had designed an **armoured car** which was mainly used in the desert battles of the Middle East. It could travel at 88 kilometres per hour and was armed with 8 mm machine guns.

Air and sea

In 1914 France had about 1500 military **aircraft**, Germany had 1000 and Britain had 179. These planes had top speeds of about 110 kilometres per hour. It was only five years since Blériot had become the first person to fly the Channel. By 1918 top speeds had doubled and in 1919 a British plane crossed the Atlantic.

German airships, called **zeppelins**, were common at the start of the war. They were like huge balloons driven by up to six engines. Balloons had been used in wars for over a century. The zeppelins were up to 200 metres long and could stay in the air for days. Although coastal towns had been bombarded by German ships before this, people inland were safe from attack. Now, for the first

Source G

'Warneford's Great Exploit', painted by Gordon Crosby in 1918.

Source H

At 3 a.m. today Flight Sub-Lieutenant R. A. J. Warneford, RN attacked a zeppelin in the air between Ghent and Brussels (Belgium) at 6,000 feet. He dropped six bombs, and the airship exploded, fell to the ground and burned. The force of the explosion caused the Morane monoplane to turn upside-down. The pilot succeeded in righting the machine, but had to make a forced landing in enemy country. However, he was able to restart his engine, and returned safely to the aerodrome.

An Admiralty announcement made on 7 June 1915. Warneford was in the Royal Navy. Planes were not yet considered important enough for there to be a separate air force.

Source I

A German Albatross fighter plane.

time, an enemy could attack British civilians without invading the country. London was bombed on 31 May 1915.

Zeppelins crossed the Channel 202 times in all, dropped 200 tonnes of bombs and killed over 500 people. **Blackouts** were enforced in British towns for the first time ever. But the large, slow-moving zeppelins were vulnerable to attack. They were frightening, but not very effective.

The first military aeroplanes were used only for observation of enemy troop movements. But soon machine guns, bombs and even torpedoes were fitted, and **air combat** became more common. In July 1915, a German aircraft designer called **Anthony Fokker** made a machine gun which was synchronized with the plane's propeller, so that it could shoot straight ahead through the blades. 'Dogfights' between rival aircraft were spectacular and, without parachutes, very dangerous. The average life expectancy of a British pilot in 1917 was two weeks. **Baron von Richthofen** ('the Red Baron') became the most famous of the First World War pilots.

By 1918 both sides had designed **long-distance bomber planes**. The German Gotha bombers killed over 850 people in air raids in 1918. Britain sent Hanley Page bombers to raid Germany. Yet it is doubtful whether air power affected the outcome of the war.

The advances in **battleship design** have been described in Unit 2.5. The changes were improvements to existing ideas rather than totally new technologies. But this war did bring the first widespread use of **submarines**. They could travel at speed on the surface, had deck-mounted artillery and could also use their electric engines to travel under water. Their main weapon was the torpedo. The German U9 (a type of submarine) had four 43 cm torpedo tubes. German U-boats almost cut off Britain's food supply in 1917.

Questions

Section A

1 a List all the different types of sources which are used in this unit to illustrate weapons used in the First World War.
  b What other types of sources could an historian use to study First World War weapons?

2 Look at Sources G and H. How reliable do you think they are?

Section B

3 a Describe the new weapons used in the First World War.
  b How far had methods of fighting in the First World War changed in comparison with earlier wars?

4 'Change is not always an improvement.' How far does the development of weapons in the First World War support this statement?

Source J

A British K-class submarine of the time.

2.7 Revolution in Russia

Stalemate on the Eastern Front

Russia was ruled by an emperor called Tsar Nicholas. The people had little power. The Tsar was the head of the government and the leader of the armed forces. At first the war was popular. The Russians felt that Germany had attacked without reason, so they supported the war and the Tsar.

But the armies on the Eastern Front had soon become bogged down in trench warfare. The Tsar wasn't a successful war leader. The Russian economy could not stand a long drawn-out war. Military supplies clogged up the roads and railways. Over 15 million men joined the army and without these workers, industrial production fell. In 1915 almost 600 factories and mills closed down. Men and horses were also taken from the farms. Food supplies began to run out.

Political unrest

It seemed as if the Tsar could not run the economy properly. Businesses were going bankrupt. Shortages sent prices up, so even those in work suffered. Workers began to strike in protest. There were almost 1600 strikes in 1916. The army were brought in to put down demonstrations by the strikers.

Socialist and Communist groups blamed the Tsar for the country's problems. They wanted a new form of government controlled by the people. They encouraged the strikes. By the end of 1916, it was only the strength of the army which kept the Tsar in power.

But the army was in turmoil. Over 3.5 million Russian soldiers had died and conditions at the front were appalling. Men began to desert. Soldiers in the cities refused to put down the demonstrations. In March 1917, 150,000 troops in Petrograd deserted. The workers there took control of the arsenal and seized 40,000 rifles. Councils of workers and soldiers called **soviets** took control of the cities. Tsar Nicholas abdicated. This was the **March Revolution**.

Source A

No one knows the figures of Russian losses. Five or eight million? All we know is that sometimes in our battles with Russians we had to remove mounds of enemy corpses before our trenches in order to get a clear field of fire against fresh attacks.

General Hindenberg commenting in 1916.

Source B

A German cartoon dated July 1917. Lloyd George, the British Prime Minister, President Wilson of the USA, and Ribot, Prime Minister of France, turn their backs on Tsar Nicholas. He looks on sadly at his former friends.

The Bolshevik Revolution

The Allies did not approve of the revolution. But they needed Russia's support. They turned their backs on the Tsar and supported the new Russian government, led by **Kerensky**. This government agreed to fight on and force Germany from Russian soil. But the war continued to go badly. Morale fell again. Over 100,000 soldiers deserted in April 1917. In the cities, food prices continued to rise.

Gradually the soviets in the cities fell under the control of Communists called **Bolsheviks**. The Bolsheviks had popular policies. They promised to withdraw from the war. They said that the people would rule Russia. Workers would control the factories and the land would be divided up among the peasants. They had their own private army of 20,000 men called the **Red Guard**. In November 1917, their leader, **Vladimir Lenin**, came to Petrograd. The Red Guard arrested the government ministers. Lenin became the country's leader. This was the **October Revolution**.

Lenin withdrew Russia from the war. By March 1918, he had signed a peace treaty with Germany called the **Treaty of Brest Litovsk**. Russia took no further part in the First World War.

Source C

The soldiers, workers and peasants of Russia did not overthrow the government of the Tsar and Kerensky merely to become cannon fodder for allied imperialism.

Trotsky, a Bolshevik leader, refusing the pleas of the Allies to continue the fight against Germany, 1917.

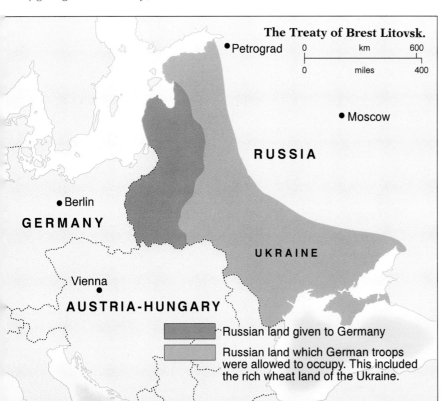

Source D

The Bolsheviks came to power in Russia, promising economic and political reforms. This Russian poster from 1920 shows that Lenin also wanted to sweep the kings, capitalists and priests from the rest of the globe.

Questions

Section A

1 Explain the following terms:
   ● Tsar   ● soviets   ● Bolsheviks.

2 Look at Source D. It is a Russian poster showing Lenin, the leader of the Bolsheviks. What does the poster tell us about Bolshevik policies?

3 a Why was the withdrawal of Russia from the war such a blow to the Allies?
   b 'Source B shows how badly they needed Russia's support.' Explain this statement.

Section B

4 Explain why the Tsar became unpopular and was overthrown. Use the following headings to help you:
   ● economic reasons
   ● military reasons
   ● political reasons.

5 'Military failure was the main reason for the overthrow of the Tsar.' How far do you agree with this statement?

2.8 The USA Enters the War

A poster from the US recruitment campaign in 1917. The picture shows a mother and baby drowning after a U-boat attack.

In the early 20th century the population of the **United States of America** was made up largely of **immigrants** and their descendants. They had come from all over Europe, including Britain, Germany, Austria and Italy. In 1914 the US President **Woodrow Wilson** said, 'We have to be **neutral**. Otherwise our mixed population would wage war on each other.'

Many Americans, including Wilson, wanted the Allies to win the war. They preferred their democratic governments to the old-fashioned rule of the aristocratic families of Germany and Austria-Hungary. But, above all, they wanted **isolation** from European affairs. This war did not seem to be any concern of theirs.

Wilson tried hard to maintain this neutrality. American bankers were allowed to lend money both to the Allies and to the Central Powers. But neutrality was not simple. For example, the Allies asked the USA to supply **raw materials**, **food** and **weapons**. Should a neutral power be allowed to do this?

Artists' comments on the policy of the USA towards the First World War in the years 1914–17, before it joined the Allies. One picture was drawn for an American magazine, one for a British and one for a German. In Source C, President Wilson is saying to the American Eagle, 'Gee, what a dove I've made out of you!'

Wilson decided that both sides should be able to send ships to buy US goods. Because the British dominated the seas, they could send merchant ships; Germany couldn't. From 1915 to 1917 one-third of all British shells used were bought from the USA. This did not seem neutral to the Germans.

Germany struck at this Atlantic trade with **U-boats**, but it was not only British sailors who drowned. In 1915, 124 Americans died on the *Lusitania*. This enraged the American public. Wilson warned the Germans that he could not stay neutral long if they kept up the U-boat attacks. The German attacks had to be reduced. This also did not seem very neutral to the Germans.

This uneasy neutrality lasted until 1917. Two things happened to change it. The first, in February, was the renewal by the German navy of unrestricted submarine warfare. Germany was becoming desperate to find a way to win the war and wanted to starve Britain into submission. In March 1917 four US ships were sunk.

That same month, the **Zimmerman telegram** came to light. Arthur Zimmerman was the German Foreign Minister. On 1 March, Britain released to the US press copies of a telegram from Zimmerman to the German Embassy in Mexico City. It told the German Ambassador there to offer an alliance with Mexico and encourage Mexico to declare war on the USA.

On 2 April, Wilson advised **Congress** (the US parliament) to declare war on Germany. He said that the USA had to crusade to 'make the world safe for democracy'. Members of Congress were so enthusiastic that many leaped to their feet, cheering. The American public were just as keen, and on 6 April 1917 the USA entered the First World War by declaring war on Germany.

The support of the USA was a huge boost to Allied morale at a time when it was badly needed. Allied efforts at the Somme and Verdun in 1916 had caused huge losses; the Nivelle offensive was failing; Russia had just been crippled by revolution; German submarines threatened to starve Britain.

But the impact of the USA entering the war is often exaggerated. The Allies were already buying much of their war materials from the USA, and the declaration of war made little difference to this. Also, the USA had to recruit and train its army from almost nothing, and then had to ship its forces almost 5000 kilometres away. It was Spring 1918 before they arrived in any numbers in Europe.

Source E

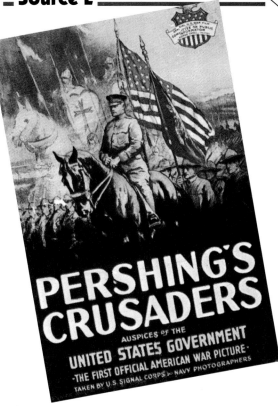

A poster sent ahead of the US troops to boost morale in Britain in 1917. It gives a clear idea of how the USA viewed its entry into the war.

Questions

Section A

1 Why did the USA remain neutral at the start of the First World War?

2 Why did the USA enter the war in 1917?

Section B

3 Study Sources B, C and D carefully.
   a What do you think each source is saying about President Wilson and US policy?
   b Which source do you think is from a US magazine of the time and which ones from British and German magazines?
   c All the sources are saying different things about the USA. Does this make them useless to historians?

4 Study Sources A and E.
   a What do they tell you about:
      ● why the USA entered the war?
      ● the uniforms of US soldiers?
      ● the US flag in 1917?
   b Which is the most valuable to historians, Source A or Source E? Give reasons for your answers.

2.9 *The War Ends*

The German war machine was breaking down by 1917. Royal Navy **blockades** of German ports were cutting off essential supplies of rubber, oil and metals. German troops and war supplies could no longer be sent to support Germany's allies. The return to unlimited submarine warfare in February 1917 was a final attempt to starve Britain into surrender. But as we have seen it only made matters worse by bringing the USA into the war in April. Faced with this desperate situation, the Germans instructed **General Ludendorff** to launch an all-out attack on the Western Front in March 1918.

The attack was successful at first. The Germans broke through the Allied trenches and gained about 65 kilometres in ten days. It was the biggest breakthrough since the first days of the war. But the Germans lacked the troops and armoured transport to press home their advantage. The Allies regrouped under the control of one supreme commander, the French **Marshal Foch**. As in 1914, the German advance was halted at the River Marne.

The Allies counter-attacked using tanks in August 1918. Many of these vehicles broke down, and they were vulnerable to armour-piercing bullets. Even so, they demoralized the German troops, who retreated to the **Hindenburg Line**. This was a new area of defences, complete with concrete bunkers and machine-gun posts, all protected by fields of barbed wire. Helped by their tank superiority, the Allies pushed on until they had broken through.

The armistice: 11 November 1918

In Berlin, the politicians and generals could see that the situation was hopeless. An epidemic of **influenza** had added to the problems of the German people. Over 1700 Berliners died in one day. There were **revolutionary uprisings** in Munich and Berlin, and a **naval mutiny** at Kiel. **Greece** had finally joined the Allies. This helped the offensive against **Bulgaria**, which surrendered in September. In October 1918 the British troops in the Middle East forced **Turkey** to surrender. On 4 November, following defeat by the Italians at Vittorio Veneto, **Austria** signed a ceasefire.

The situation was so grave that **Kaiser William abdicated** on 9 November and fled to Holland. The German army remained undefeated, but its government had no alternative but to surrender. An **armistice** (ceasefire) was agreed, starting at 11 a.m. on the eleventh day of the eleventh month of 1918. This is the day celebrated every year on Remembrance Sunday (Poppy Day).

_Source A

We had no tanks. Armoured cars were equally absent, and so were the motorized machine guns (mounted on motorcycle sidecars) which the British had.

A German soldier recalling the German offensive of 1918.

_Source B

American recruiting poster.

_Source C

Their effects were largely on morale. They did a good job in crushing machine-gun posts and in village fighting. The infantry liked them, and the enemy evidently stood in fear of them.

Brigadier-General Sir J. E. Edmonds, a British commander in 1918, describing the Allies' use of tanks.

Source D

> We have no meat or potatoes. Fat is unobtainable. The shortage is so great that it is a mystery to me what the people of Berlin live on. The workers say, 'Better a horrible end than an endless horror.'

A German minister commenting in October 1918.

Source E

> This is the worst-ever day for the German army. We have nearly reached the limit of our powers. The war must be ended.

The German General Ludendorff, reporting the failure of his offensive in August 1918.

Source F

> 'Your Majesty, the advance has been stopped. We have lost the war'.

General Von Moltke's conclusion after the failure of the German offensive in 1914.

Questions

Section A

1 Mark your timeline of the war with the key events at the end of the war.

2 a Why did the Germans launch their final attack in March 1918?

b Why did it fail?

3 a Find out the population of the town or city where you live. Compare it to the losses in the major battles of the First World War.

b Study the diagram showing casualties in the First World War. What would have been the likely outcome if all of your class had volunteered to fight in the war?

Section B

Here is a list of possible reasons why Germany lost the war:
- Trying to fight on two fronts for too long.
- The British blockade of German ports.
- Entry of the USA into the war.
- The Allies' superiority in tank warfare.

4 a Using the text and sources in this unit to help you, list the reasons above in order of importance and explain your answer.

b Put yourself in the place of first President Wilson, then General Ludendorff, then Marshal Foch, and reconsider the list for each of them. Are all of your lists the same? If not, why not?

5 'Once the Schlieffen Plan (page 10) had failed, Germany was bound to lose.' Do you agree with this statement? Explain your answer.

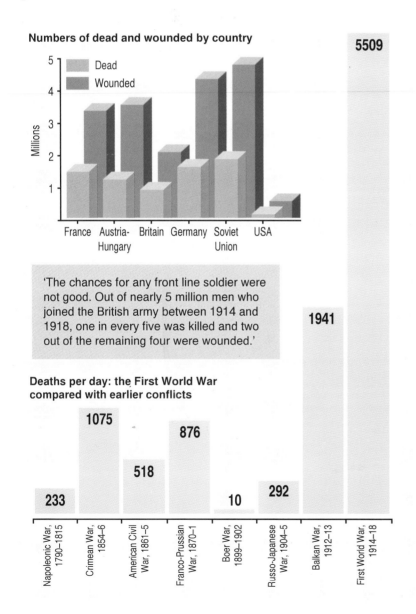

Numbers of dead and wounded by country

(Legend: Dead, Wounded)

France, Austria-Hungary, Britain, Germany, Soviet Union, USA — 5509

> 'The chances for any front line soldier were not good. Out of nearly 5 million men who joined the British army between 1914 and 1918, one in every five was killed and two out of the remaining four were wounded.'

Deaths per day: the First World War compared with earlier conflicts

War	Deaths per day
Napoleonic War, 1790–1815	233
Crimean War, 1854–6	1075
American Civil War, 1861–5	518
Franco-Prussian War, 1870–1	876
Boer War, 1899–1902	10
Russo-Japanese War, 1904–5	292
Balkan War, 1912–13	1941
First World War, 1914–18	5509

Casualties in the First World War.

3.1 The Home Front

Civilians in danger

For the first time in Britain's history, it was not just the troops who were in danger. In the very first days of the war German **ships** bombarded coastal towns. When Hartlepool and Scarborough were shelled, 500 people were killed or injured. Later, **zeppelins** and then **Gotha bombers** made regular air raids. Over 1000 people were killed, with 3300 more injured. This was a new and frightening experience for the British public.

Precautions seem primitive by later standards. **Blackouts** were ordered at night, but they were not very effective. There were no air-raid sirens because the government thought that they would cause panic or encourage people to stop work. When bombing raids were expected, police officers cycled the streets clearing people away.

The nation's leaders

The war needed the full commitment of the whole of British society. Other disagreements had to be forgotten. Trade unions which were planning strikes in 1914 put them aside in the national interest. Unrest in Ireland subsided for a while. Political parties agreed to forget their differences.

When the war started, the **Liberal Party** was in power. The Prime Minister was **Herbert Asquith**. **David Lloyd George** was Chancellor of the Exchequer, **Winston Churchill** was in charge at the Admiralty, and **Lord Kitchener** became Secretary for War. In May 1915 Asquith created a **coalition government** inviting leaders of the other main parties into the government. The Conservatives **Andrew Bonar Law** and **Arthur Balfour** and the Labour leader **Arthur Henderson** all became ministers.

As the war dragged on without victory, people became dissatisfied with some of the ministers, but not with Lloyd George: he was the most dynamic of them all. He became Minister of Munitions in 1915 and then moved to head the War Office. In December 1916

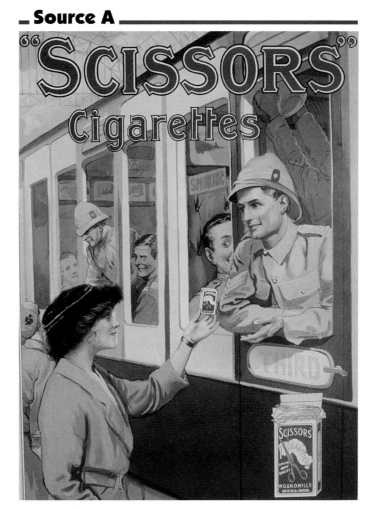

Source A

A wartime cigarette advertisement. The war was so much at the centre of people's lives that advertisers used military themes to give extra appeal to products ranging from chocolate to soap.

Asquith resigned during a political squabble. The King asked Lloyd George to be Prime Minister.

The change was good for Britain. Lloyd George appointed a **war cabinet** of only five ministers. He distrusted the advice of military experts and often overruled them. He led the government with huge energy. He was personally behind the **convoy system** and was a strong supporter of **conscription** (see Unit 3.5). Bonar Law said, 'He thought of nothing and aimed at nothing and hoped for nothing but a successful end to the war.'

The change of government was bad for the Liberal Party, which was split between Asquith and Lloyd George. The Liberals did very badly in the general election of 1918. It is important to note that war in Britain did not weaken **parliamentary government**. The violent swings to extreme political groups which occurred in Europe, especially Russia and Germany, did not happen in Britain. The **Labour Party** had been able to share government in the coalitions. It remained quite moderate, and improved its vote in 1918.

DORA

During the war, the government passed laws to give itself new powers to improve the war effort. For example, on 8 August 1914 the government passed the **Defence of the Realm Act** (known as **DORA**). Some of its new regulations were predictable: suspected spies could be imprisoned without trial; hoarding food and profiteering were to be punished by stiff prison sentences; newspapers were censored; and the government took control of the mines and railways. But many of the DORA restrictions affected ordinary people. For example, the Act limited the powers of trade unions, and gave the government power to control all rents and prices and to seize private property, such as land and horses.

Some regulations introduced by DORA changed **everyday routines**. In 1916, for the first time, people had to put their clocks forward one hour to create an extra hour of summer daylight for workers. The government was also worried about the effects of drink on workers and troops on leave. The opening hours for public houses were reduced and beer and spirits were watered down. 'Treating', or buying drinks in rounds, was made illegal. Drink prices were also increased. The King gave up drinking alcohol as a good example to the people. All of this reduced the consumption of alcohol. Convictions for drunkenness fell from 3388 in 1914 to 449 in 1918. Some people argued that alcoholic drinks should be banned altogether.

Source B

A poster of a group favouring the abolition of alcoholic drinks.

Source C

DORA made all of the following illegal:
- writing letters in code
- spreading rumours about the war
- using a camera without a permit
- lighting bonfires and fireworks
- flying kites
- buying binoculars
- feeding bread to dogs, poultry, pigeons or horses
- trespassing on railways or railway bridges
- ringing church bells.

Activities banned by the 1914 Defence of the Realm Act.

Money, work and attitudes

The government needed large sums of **money** to pay for ships, tanks and artillery, the wages of the troops and their uniforms, weapons and food. By 1917 Britain was spending £5.7 million per day on the war. Taxes were increased. **Income tax** rose from 9d (about 4p) to 6 shillings (30p) in the pound for the wealthy – which was very high by standards of the time. Britain also borrowed money from the USA and encouraged people to lend all of their savings to the government by buying **war bonds**.

Another change was **inflation**. Prices of some goods doubled and even trebled during the war. This was caused partly by the government borrowing and partly by shortages of goods. Unit 3.4 describes the **rationing** which had to be introduced in 1916.

Industry and **farming** also had to change to meet the needs of the country (see Units 3.2 and 3.3). More and more **women** worked in all kinds of jobs previously done by men. This caused a change in **social attitudes**, especially in the behaviour and expectations of women. Women began to gain in confidence and independence, for example, changing their style of clothes, wearing trousers, smoking in public and visiting pubs.

People's **sexual behaviour** changed too. Illegitimate births increased during the war, and there were over 50,000 cases of syphilis among soldiers by 1916. In 1918 Dr Marie Stopes issued a book calling for more advice about contraception. Sexual behaviour began to be openly discussed for the first time.

Source D

Victoria Station in wartime. Before the war Britain had a very small army. By 1916 the streets were full of soldiers.

Source E

A First World War poster advertising war loans.

Source F

I arrived at the cottage that morning to find his mother and sister, standing in hopeless distress in the midst of his returned kit, which was lying, just opened, all over the floor. The garments sent back included the outfit that he had been wearing when he was hit – the tunic torn back and front by the bullet, the khaki vest dark and stiff with blood.

The writer Vera Brittain describing the scene shortly after hearing that her fiancé had been killed in France.

Source G

I remember my mother going pale one afternoon as she saw a telegram boy coming towards the house. She smiled as he cycled past, but she didn't say a word. My father and brother were in the navy, and you never knew if the telegram might be for you.

Recollections of Mabel Bell, who was 14 years old when the war broke out.

Children in the war

The **Boy Scouts** movement had been founded in 1908, and the **Girl Guides** in 1909. Now they were put to work. The 150,000 Scouts helped to bring in the harvests, carried messages between government departments and served in soup kitchens. They were also asked to guard railway bridges, telegraph poles and reservoirs at night. Girl Guides cared for the old, looked after refugee children from abroad and knitted socks and gloves for the troops.

One unpleasant change was in the role of the telegram boys. In an age without telephones in homes, urgent news was delivered by young **telegram messengers** on bicycles. During the war, a visit from the telegram boy usually meant news of the death of a relative. Most families suffered. The son of Asquith, the Prime Minister, was killed in battle.

As well as working, however, children continued to go to **school.** The government realized the value of better-educated workers and soldiers. The number of children at secondary school increased from 180,000 in 1914 to 220,000 in 1917, and the school leaving age for all children was raised to 14 in 1918.

After the war

The whole country had pulled together to win the war. This changed people's expectations of life. They all expected to share the rewards of victory. All men over 21 and most women over 30 were **given the vote** in 1918. People wanted to make sure that the world they lived in after the war was worth all the suffering. They expected **social reform** to create a Britain 'fit for heroes'. More voters turned to the Labour Party, and the Liberal Party went into decline. But the country's hopes were in vain. As it turned out, the 1920s were a decade of depression and disappointment for most of Britain.

Source H

A picture from the 1920s showing fashion for the young. Daring young women wore short, knee-length skirts and plunging necklines. Some people began to worry that the young were adopting 'loose behaviour' – and not only in Britain. In 1920 the US city of Chicago made clothes like these illegal, with fines of $10 to $100 for offenders.

Questions

Section A

1 a Copy the items on this list which were features of the Home Front during the First World War:
air raids   blackouts
four-minute warnings   coalitions
DORA   Winston Churchill
Adolf Hitler   conscription
prohibition   rationing
income tax   telegrams.

   b Write a sentence about each item.

2 Look at Source C. Why do you think each of these things was made illegal?

Section B

3 Describe the changes which took place in Britain during the war, using the following headings:
● political changes   ● economic changes
● social changes.

4 a Find an example of change which could be described as progress.

   b Find one example of change which was not progress.

   c Explain your choice.

5 'The First World War totally changed people's lives.' How far do you agree with this statement?

3.2 Industry

In 1914 the government took control of **key industries** such as mining and the railways. This had never been done before in Britain, but British industry had two big problems.

The first problem was a **shortage of workers**. Many skilled workers joined the army. The trade unions did not want unskilled workers to replace them. They called this '**dilution**' of skills. They thought it would devalue skilled jobs and reduce wages. In March 1915 Lloyd George, then Chancellor of the Exchequer, made an agreement with the unions. Dilution was accepted, but things would return to normal after the war. Strikes were outlawed. This cleared the way for gaps in manufacturing industries to be filled by unskilled men and by a large increase in women workers (see Unit 3.8).

Source A

Trade unionists objected that women would lower men's wages. Yet women were paid less than men. In the national shell factories, the top wage for men was £4 6s 6d [about £4.32]; that for women was £2 4s 6d [about £2.22]. By the end of 1915 the munitions plants were employing three times as many women as men. At one Croydon factory the women who replaced men earning £3 per week received 12s 6d [about 62p].

From Lloyd George's memoirs.

A wartime government poster describing the achievements of the munitions (weapons) industry.

Source B

THE WAR OF MUNITIONS

HOW GREAT BRITAIN HAS MOBILISED HER INDUSTRIES

Source C

A painting entitled 'For King and Country', by Edward Skinner, showing women working in a munitions factory.

The second problem was that industry could not supply **key war materials**. Most British factories were still small craft workshops. There was little **mass production** on the conveyor-belt system used in many factories in the USA. Britain also lacked many key industries; an explosives industry, for example. Germany had supplied its pre-war needs. Britain had also relied upon the German and US **machine tools** industries to make machines for factories. This caused difficulties when it came to setting up new factories to make artillery, lorries and aeroplanes.

Lloyd George tackled these problems when he became **Minister of Munitions** in May 1915. First, he arranged for supplies from the USA. But he also gave British companies money to enable them to change to munitions production. He financed new '**national factories**' which manufactured products for the war effort. In 1915, 73 of these opened; there were 218 by 1918. By 1917 Britain supplied weapons not only to France and Italy, but even to US troops.

Lloyd George also ensured that **welfare** went with warfare. The national factories had canteens, nurseries and rest-rooms. All munitions workers were covered by National Insurance, which gave pensions and health insurance.

The war helped **innovation in industry**. British designers improved existing ideas for the war effort. Rolls-Royce improved the petrol engine and built swift new armoured cars (see Unit 2.6). Hanley Page improved aircraft design. British designers came up with entirely new products; the tank, for example, was an invention of British industry.

Questions

Section A

1 a What were the main problems which British industry faced at the beginning of the war?

b Using the text and Sources B and C, explain how industry overcame these problems.

2 The trade unions feared 'dilution of skills'.
  a What does this mean?
  b Read Source A. According to this source, did the fears of the trade unionists come true?

Section B

3 'Lloyd George single-handedly transformed the munitions industry and provided a sound supply of weapons, ammunition and equipment for the armed forces.' Do you agree with this statement? Explain your answer.

3.3 Farming on the Home Front

A wartime government poster.

In 1914 Britain **imported** most of its food; but British farms produced large quantities, too. The government was keen to make sure that farming was as efficient as other major industries. This became even more important as German U-boats started to attack ships bringing grain to Britain. There were rumours of food shortages by 1916, and food queues started to appear in 1918.

Like other industries during the war, farming had a **shortage of workers** when men joined the army. The government helped here. In 1915 the Board of Education allowed **children** to miss school to help farmers. The **Women's Land Army** was set up to provide female labour. Even some **prisoners of war** worked in the fields. The use of lorries and tractors was encouraged to save labour.

The government also used its powers to reorganize farm production. It encouraged production of **staple foods**, such as grain and potatoes, rather than luxury foods like meat. In 1916 **War Agricultural Committees** were set up. These encouraged the use of allotments and organized the ploughing of parks and playing fields for planting. In 1917 the **Corn Production Act** was passed. This encouraged farmers to grow grain by guaranteeing minimum prices for their produce. Some farmers were made to plough up their pastures and plant grain instead.

Source B

1900–9	5.1 million tons
1910–19	5.2 million tons

Imports of wheat and flour, 1900–19.

Source C

Year	Europe	North America	Australia	Other
1900–9	16%	40%	8%	36%
1910–19	8%	57%	10%	25%

The origin of Britain's wheat imports, 1900–19.

Source D

1910–14	5d [about 2p]
1915–19	9d [about 4p]

Average London prices of a large loaf, 1910–19.

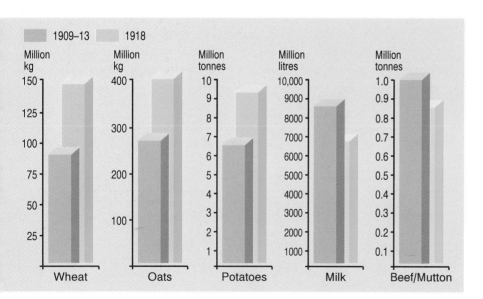

Changes in farming, 1913–18.

Source E

'A Land Girl Ploughing', by Cecil Aldin. By 1917 there were over 260,000 women in the Land Army.

Source F

Cheap imported food made many farmers give up producing wheat before the war. By 1914 only 20 per cent of wheat was home grown. This nearly led to disaster in the war. In the winter of 1916–17 there was less than six weeks' food in the country. The German fleet blocked the way to Russian and American wheat. In 1917 the government tackled the main problem, the shortage of grain. Through the Corn Production Act it gave help to farmers who grew grain crops. By 1919 they were growing 60 per cent rather than 20 per cent of Britain's wheat.

From John Robottom, 'A Social and Economic History of Britain', 1986.

Source G

Food prices rose during the war, but there was no great concern except for a short time after 1917 when one out of every four merchant ships failed to make it back to British ports. This hit grain supplies for a while. The government had several solutions. A convoy system was introduced to protect shipping; food distribution was improved; people were encouraged not to waste food; and steps were taken to boost farming output at home. Less grain was used in brewing.

Rationing was not necessary until 1918. Not only did rationing and other controls prevent starvation, there is also evidence that the diet of the nation improved. An official survey found that there were fewer than half as many undernourished schoolchildren in 1918 as there had been in 1913. There were similar results in Birmingham, Bolton, Bradford, Bristol, Glasgow and Nottingham.

From Trevor May, 'An Economic and Social History of Britain, 1760–1970', 1987.

Questions

Section A

1 Use the text and sources in this unit to answer the following questions.
   a What changes were there to British food **production** during the war?
   b What changes were there to food **imports** during the war?

Section B

2 What do Sources F and G say about
   a food shortages during the war?
   b food imports?
   c the measures taken to tackle food shortages during the war?

3 What impression do Sources F and G give about the importance of Britain's farmers in preventing food shortages?

4 Look at Sources A and E. Do they support any statements in Sources F and G?

5 Sources F and G are both extracts from modern textbooks. They both give interpretations of the food supply during the war. Which is the better interpretation of the food supply situation? Explain your answer.

3.4 Rationing

The war **disrupted food supplies**. U-boat raids on merchant ships made food imports less reliable. Shipping losses were worse at some times than at others. Farmers gradually changed the food they produced as the war went on, and this also affected food supplies. Some people hoarded food, which caused shortages in the shops. Many prices went up; for example the price of meat rose by 40 per cent during the war. This made some of the food which was available too expensive for people to buy regularly. The government gradually took action to reduce this disruption of food supplies.

Government action

The government started an **advertising campaign** to persuade people to be careful. This lasted the whole of the war. 'One teaspoonful of breadcrumbs saved by each person each day makes 40,000 tons of bread a year,' said one poster. The government reduced the amount of wheat used in **brewing**. It also used the law – DORA (see Unit 3.1) – to make wasting food illegal. A Welsh lady who fed meat to her St Bernard dog was fined £20. A man who showed what he thought of his dinner by throwing it on the fire at work was fined £10.

A poster from 1917.

Source A

We risk our lives to bring you food. It's up to you not to waste it.

'A Message from our Seamen'

Source B

Queues before breakfast were the features of yesterday's shopping. The horse butchers in Soho were crowded with French, Belgian and Russian women. Grocers' shops were selling tinned milk at the record price of 1s 6d [7.5p] per tin.

From the 'Daily Mirror', 15 January, 1918.

Source C

My father was made Food Controller in 1917. During January and February 1918 as many as a million people were standing in queues for food. The food often all went before the last could get their share. There were butter and margarine queues, meat queues and, a new development, fish queues. On 25 February 1918 the rationing plan started.

Viscountess Rhondda recalling the war years.

Source D

A rather special First World War rationing card.

The government also took control of food supplies and distribution. From 1915 to the end of the war it bought the entire meat exports from Australia and New Zealand. Official stocks of sugar, wheat, meat and hides were stored in **government warehouses**. These were only released for sale at controlled times and prices. There were constant rumours about stocks of food running low. Some food, such as meat and fish, became hard to buy. Some butchers started to open for only a few hours a day and then sold out. But bread, potatoes and other staple foods were always available.

Despite this, in January 1918 food queues appeared. People complained of shortages in the shops, and there was evidence of increased hoarding. The government finally decided on **official rationing,** which included meat, sugar, butter and eggs, for the whole country. It was the fairest way to ensure that everyone had enough but no one kept too much.

Every household was given a **food card** or ration card. This allowed people to buy small amounts of meat and groceries each week. The amounts varied for different types and ages of people and with the time of year and shipping losses. A typical weekly allowance per person was 141 grams of butter and 567 grams of meat (measured at that time in ounces, not grams). Bread, the staple food of the poor, was never rationed.

Source E

The food position was in fact better than it had been earlier. The wheat harvest for 1917 was the best of the century. Yet for some reason people took alarm and bought food irrationally. There were disappointed queues at every grocer's and butcher's shop. Rationing started. This was not to reduce consumption of food. The ration book was more a promise that all reasonable demands would be met.

From A. J. P. Taylor, 'English History 1914–45', 1965.

Questions

Section A

1 Look at Source A.
   a What message is it giving?
   b How does the poster try to make sure that people take notice of this message?

2 The following list shows how much food per person per week could be bought on a typical ration card. How does it compare with what you eat each week?

   8 oz of sugar
   5 oz of butter or margarine
   2 oz of tea
   4 oz of jam
   8 oz of bacon
   20 oz of other meat
   (1 oz = approximately 28 grams.)

3 What can you learn from the ration card shown in Source D?

Section B

4 How did government methods of controlling food supplies change during the war?

5 'The change in food supply during the war was very simple. The longer the war went on, the worse the situation got.' How far do you agree with this statement? Give reasons for your answer.

3.5 Recruitment to the Armed Forces

When the war started, Britain had a small well-trained army of just 100,000 men. It was obvious that a much bigger army would be needed to win the war. The Liberal government, however, was against **conscription** (forcing people to join the forces), as it believed this went against an individual's freedom. It was decided to call for men to **volunteer** for the army. This had always worked in the past.

Lord Kitchener, a national hero at the time, was made the Minister for War and given the task of recruiting for the army. To begin with, swept along by **patriotism**, thousands of men volunteered. So many came forward that the authorities could hardly cope. It seems that nobody had realized that the recruits would need housing, clothing and weapons. There were not even enough government clerks to do all the paperwork.

These problems were partly solved when local councils around the country started to raise battalions of volunteers based on local loyalties. Such groups were called **pals' battalions** – the Leeds Pals was just one of many.

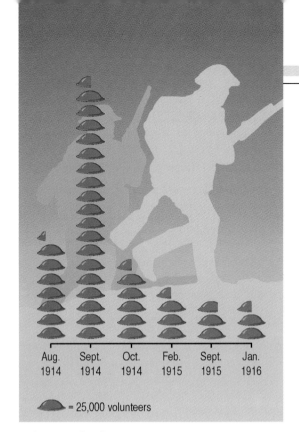

Aug. 1914   Sept. 1914   Oct. 1914   Feb. 1915   Sept. 1915   Jan. 1916

= 25,000 volunteers

Volunteers for the army, 1914–1916 (selected months).

Source A

Source B

BRITONS

"WANTS" YOU

JOIN YOUR COUNTRY'S ARMY!

GOD SAVE THE KING

Reproduced by permission of LONDON OPINION

A recruiting poster from 1914.

Volunteers outside a recruiting office in 1915.

There was also the problem of keeping industry going at home. Many of the men joining up were skilled workers who were really needed to work in **key industries** such as shipbuilding and coal-mining.

Registration and conscription

In August 1915 **National Registration** was introduced. Men between the ages of 18 and 41 had to fill in a form giving their personal details. The government discovered that there were 5 million men who had not joined up, 3 million of whom were married and 2 million single. Out of the single men about 600,000 were working in essential industries and therefore needed at home. This still left 1.4 million single men who had not joined up. Many people started to wonder why this was so.

In May 1916, a few weeks before the planned attack on the Germans at the Somme, the government introduced conscription. All men aged between 18 and 41 had to join the army unless they were working in essential industries.

Source C

There is evidence to show that events in France and Belgium had an influence on recruitment. Recruiting returns rose sharply after the retreat from Mons.

From Peter Simkins, 'Kitchener's Army', 1988. The Battle of Mons, at the end of August 1914, saw the British Expeditionary Force pushed back by the German army.

Source D

We were fighting for king, country and empire, and for 'gallant little Belgium'. The British Empire was the greatest empire the world had ever known. Its greatness was due to the superior qualities of the British.

Ulric Nisbet, speaking after the war. Nisbet attended Marlborough School, then joined the army in 1914 as a junior officer.

Source E

The war was the only effective way to protect Britain from unemployment caused by the dumping of cheap German goods in this country.

G.W. Evans, an army volunteer in 1914, commenting after the war.

Source F

I was sick of a humdrum life that led nowhere and promised nothing.

A Yorkshire farm labourer explaining why he joined up.

Source G

I was working a three-day week and drawing three days' dole money. One day someone suggested we should enlist. This sounded a glorious adventure.

Thomas Peers describing his reasons for joining up.

Questions

Section A

1 Write your own definitions of the following: voluntary enlistment; conscription; patriotism.

2 Why did the Liberals believe in voluntary enlistment in 1914?

3 Study the diagram on page 44. What trends can you see?

4 What was National Registration?

5 When was conscription introduced?

Section B

6 In what way might the diagram and Sources A and B be connected? Explain your answer.

7 a Why did men volunteer so readily for the army in 1914?
   b Divide their reasons (or motives) under the following headings:
      ● patriotic motives
      ● economic motives
      ● military motives
      ● social motives.
   c Explain your decisions.

8 Why did the government introduce conscription in May 1916? Make your answer as detailed as possible and try to say which reason was the most important.

3.6 Propaganda and the War

Propaganda is the deliberate spreading of information designed to make people believe in certain ideas and viewpoints. It is a form of mass persuasion. During the First World War propaganda was used to:

- persuade men to join the armed services, which needed recruits urgently
- keep people cheerful by making them believe that the war was being won
- make people hate the enemy so that they would keep their determination to win the war.

Such material was spread to mass audiences using newspapers, leaflets, posters, literature and paintings. Also, towards the end of the war, propaganda films and newsreels were being shown in cinemas. In 1917 the government set up the Department of Information to organize and control the spread of propaganda.

Source A

THE TRUTH FROM THE BRITISH ARMY–
OUR SOLDIERS OVERWHELMED BY NUMBERS
Amiens, France. 29 August 1914.
This is a pitiful story. Only by realizing what has happened can we nerve ourselves for the effort we must make to retrieve it. The first inkling I had that the Germans had penetrated far into France was this morning. Our small British force could not stand before a volume so immense. It has been scattered all over. British troops were set an impossible task. Let us not try to hush up the facts. England should realize that it should send reinforcements. Is an army of valour to be borne down by the sheer weight of numbers, while young Englishmen at home play golf and cricket? We want men and we want them now.

A report published in 'The Times' following the British retreat from Mons in 1914. Reports from the front were usually censored so that the public were only told the good things. This report caused a big row in Parliament. F. C. Green, the head of the Press Bureau, had allowed the report to be published without it being changed. He was forced to resign his post.

Source B

TERRIBLE DEATH
OF A DUMFRIES NURSE
Information has been received of brutalities by German soldiers on Nurse Grace Hume, a young woman belonging to the town. She was engaged in Red Cross work at Vilvorde Camp hospital near Brussels. An allied soldier caught two German soldiers in the act of cutting off Nurse Hume's left breast, her right one having been already cut off. The Germans were instantly killed. Nurse Hume died in terrible agony.

From a report in the 'Dumfries and Galloway Standard', 16 September 1914.

Source C

A recruiting poster released by the government, 1915.

Source D

TO THE
YOUNG WOMEN OF LONDON

Is your "Best Boy" wearing Khaki? If not don't <u>YOU</u> <u>THINK</u> he should be?

If he does not think that you and your country are worth fighting for—do you think he is <u>WORTHY</u> of you?

Don't pity the girl who is alone—her young man is probably a soldier—fighting for her and her country— and for <u>YOU</u>.

If your young man neglects his duty to his King and Country, the time may come when he will <u>NEGLECT YOU</u>.

Think it over—then ask him to

JOIN THE ARMY TO-DAY

A government poster of 1915.

Source E

RED CROSS OR IRON CROSS?

WOUNDED AND A PRISONER
OUR SOLDIER CRIES FOR WATER.
THE GERMAN "SISTER"
POURS IT ON THE GROUND BEFORE HIS EYES.

THERE IS NO WOMAN IN BRITAIN
WHO WOULD DO IT.

THERE IS NO WOMAN IN BRITAIN
WHO WILL FORGET IT.

An anti-German poster released by the government in 1915.

Source F

MISS EDITH CAVELL
MURDERED
October 12th 1915

REMEMBER!

A government poster of 1915. Edith Cavell was a British nurse working in Belgium. She was shot by the Germans for helping British soldiers escape from Belgium.

Questions

Section A

1 Write down a definition of **propaganda** and give an example of your own.

2 a Study Sources A–F. What were the various **media** used to spread information and ideas in 1914–18?
  b Would the media used be any different today? Explain your answer.

Section B

3 a Make out a chart like the one below and fill in the columns for each of the sources in this unit:

Source	The point being made	Why it was produced
A		

  b Are all the sources examples of government propaganda? Explain your answer.

4 Grace Hume (Source B) never went to Belgium. Does this mean that this newspaper article is useless to an historian? Explain your answer.

5 Is Source F reliable? Explain your answer.

6 'Only sources which are true are reliable to historians.' Using the sources in this unit explain whether you agree or disagree with this statement.

3.7 Attitudes to the War

Right from the start of the war, feelings ran high among the British people. In 1914 many were fanatical in their support of the war, but there were others who were against it. Quakers opposed the war for religious reasons; others simply believed it was wrong to kill. Two other groups who objected to the war were the **Union of Democratic Control** and the **No-Conscription Fellowship**. They were accused of being on the side of Germany, and their meetings were often disrupted by people shouting insults.

Young men seen wearing civilian clothes ('**slackers**') were abused in the streets. Some women handed them a white feather (a symbol of cowardice) as they walked by. German shopkeepers who had started businesses in England before the war had their windows smashed.

Conscientious objectors

When conscription was introduced in 1916 (see Unit 3.5) people who had a **conscientious objection** to fighting could appeal to a tribunal. The tribunals were made up of local dignitaries who usually treated the objectors with contempt. Such people hoped they would be excused from joining up. They were given the nickname '**conchies**' or '**Cuthberts**'. Altogether there were 16,000 conscientious objectors or **pacifists**. Most of them agreed to serve the government by doing ambulance work, forestry work or making roads. Even so, they were the target for abuse and insults.

A few people – 1600 men in all – were **absolutists**. They refused to have anything to do with the war. Lloyd-George declared that he would make their lives 'very hard'. They were imprisoned, and 70 of them died from the bad treatment they received.

After 1918 many people came to realize that the war had brought suffering and death on a scale never before experienced. It was only then that the views of the conscientious objectors came to be valued.

Source A

Are YOU in this?

A poster from 1915.

Source B

AN "OBJECT" LESSON

FATHER · BROTHER · MOTHER · SISTER · UNCLE · COUSIN

CONSCIENTIOUS OBJECTOR

Frank Holland

PLATE 9.   —By permission of John Bull

"This little pig stayed at home"

'This little pig stayed at home', a wartime cartoon from 'John Bull' magazine.

Source C

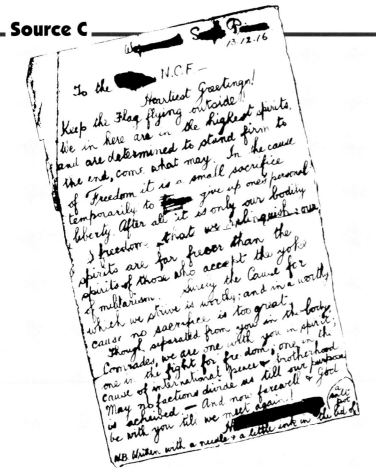

A letter smuggled out of Wormwood Scrubs prison by Harold Bing, a conscientious objector, in 1916.

Source D

A postcard about conscientious objectors dating from 1917.

Source E

The destruction of our fellow men appalls us. We cannot assist in the cutting off of one generation from life's opportunities. We deny the right of any government to make slaughter of our fellows a bounden duty.

From the manifesto of the No-Conscription Fellowship, issued in December 1914.

Source F

Conscientious objectors were, according to the popular press, 'sickly idealists', 'pasty faces' and 'curs'. They were men 'with as much pluck and brains as the rabbit and as much conscience as the skunk.'

From Christopher Martin, 'English Life in the First World War', 1974.

Questions

Section A

1 Why were white feathers often handed out to men?

2 Name two groups that were against the war.

3 What was meant by the term **conscientious objector**?

4 What did the government do with conscientious objectors?

Section B

5 a Describe the attitude to the war shown in Source A.
   b Describe the different attitudes towards conscientious objectors shown in Sources B and D.

6 'All those who objected to war did so for the same reasons.' Do you agree with this statement? Give reasons for your answer.

7 During a time of war it would be reasonable to expect a country to be united. Why, then, was there such a lot of disagreement among British people during the First World War?

3.8 The Role of Women

The status of women in society had shown signs of improving before the First World War broke out. Women had begun to work as typists in offices and it was possible for them to enter the medical profession. Despite the efforts of the **Suffragettes**, however, women were still not allowed to vote in 1914. When war broke out the Suffragettes called a truce and said that women should devote their energies to winning the war.

To begin with, the role of women was limited to knitting garments for the troops and fund-raising. Many people knew that women were capable of making a much bigger contribution. On 17 July 1915, Christabel Pankhurst organized a '**right to serve**' march in London. Also, in 1915, there was a shortage of shells on the Western Front and Lloyd-George, the Minister for Munitions, began to draft women into armaments factories. Making shells was unpleasant work; the hours were long and there was a health risk from the fumes given off by TNT. These women armaments workers were called **munitionettes** or 'canaries' because the fumes turned their skin yellow.

When conscription was introduced in 1916 there was a big demand for women to fill the workplaces left by the men. Women now began to take a wide variety of jobs. By 1917 more and more women were joining military units, such as the **Women's Army Auxiliary Corps**, to provide back-up for the troops.

In 1918 women over 30 were given the right to vote. In 1919 Nancy Astor, the first woman MP, took her seat in Parliament.

Source A

It was the war which won the vote for women. Asquith, the Prime Minister, one of the main opponents of women having the vote before the war, admitted that they had earned the vote by their own efforts. Women munitions workers, bus conductresses, land-girls, police constables and nurses all made their contribution to the war effort.

From W. O. Simpson, 'Changing Horizons: Britain 1914–80', 1986.

Source B

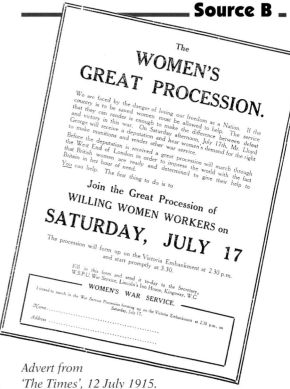

The **WOMEN'S GREAT PROCESSION.**

We are faced by the danger of losing our freedom as a Nation. If the country is to be saved women must be allowed to help. The service that they can render is enough to make the difference between defeat and victory in this war. On Saturday afternoon, July 17th, Mr. Lloyd George will receive a deputation and hear women's demand for the right to make munitions and render other war service.

Before the deputation is received a great procession will march through the West End of London in order to impress the world with the fact that British women are ready and determined to give their help to Britain in her hour of need.

You can help. The first thing to do is to

Join the Great Procession of WILLING WOMEN WORKERS on

SATURDAY, JULY 17

The procession will form up on the Victoria Embankment at 2.30 p.m. and start promptly at 3.30.

Fill in this form and send it to-day to the Secretary, W.S.P.U. War Service, Lincoln's Inn House, Kingsway, W.C.

WOMEN'S WAR SERVICE.

I intend to march in the War Service Procession forming up on the Victoria Embankment at 2.30 p.m. on Saturday, July 17.

Name ....

Address ....

Advert from 'The Times', 12 July 1915.

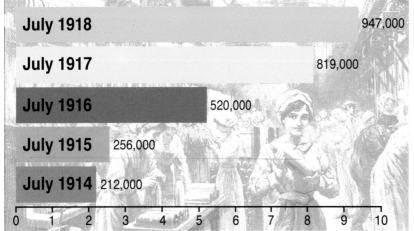

	July 1918	947,000
July 1917		819,000
July 1916	520,000	
July 1915	256,000	
July 1914	212,000	

0 1 2 3 4 5 6 7 8 9 10

The employment of women in armaments factories, 1914–18.

Occupation	1914	1918
Transport	18,000	117,000
Commerce	505,000	934,000
Agriculture	190,000	228,000
Government clerks	262,000	460,000
Domestic servants	1,650,000	1,250,000

Numbers of women employed in different occupations, 1914 and 1918.

Source C

NATIONAL SERVICE
WOMEN'S LAND ARMY

"GOD SPEED THE PLOUGH
AND THE WOMAN WHO DRIVES IT"

APPLY FOR ENROLMENT FORMS AT YOUR NEAREST POST OFFICE OR
EMPLOYMENT EXCHANGE

A Women's Land Army recruitment poster of 1917.

Source D

EXHIBITION
of WAR ECONOMY DRESS.
MUST · BE · SEEN · BY · EVERYONE
Grafton Galleries, Bond Street.
10 to 6. From 3rd to 31st August (Inclusive)

1818   1918

The National Standard Dress will be demonstrated by
Mrs Allan Hawkey, The Inventor,
who will Lecture Daily.
MANY OTHER ATTRACTIONS
Orchestra will play daily.
Admission 1/3d Inclusive of Tax.

An advertisement for an exhibition of wartime economy dress.

Source E

Their new 'wealth' brought them a new look. Powder and make-up became common; silk stockings were bought by working-class shell-girls, and they smoked openly in public.

From Christopher Martin, 'English Life in the First World War', 1974. 'Shell-girls' were munition workers.

Source F

Most Women's Land Army members already had a farming background. Farmers' wives and children had always been expected to do any job on the farm and without pay. They only needed to acquire the skill of ploughing.

From 'Hampshire in the Great War', 1985.

Source G

None of the men spoke to me, and they would give me no help as to where to find things. My drawer was nailed up, and oil was poured over everything through a crack.

Recollections of a wartime woman worker in an engineering works. From Howard Martin, 'Britain since 1800: Towards the Welfare State', 1988.

Questions

Section A

1 Draw a timeline to represent the years 1914–19. For each year, mark one key event in the changing role of women.

2 Why do you think women over 30 were given the vote in 1918?

Section B

3 Explain the changes shown by the table and the diagram on page 50.

4 Do Sources C and F show change or continuity? Explain your answer.

5 List the changes in the position of women during the First World War under the headings:
 ● social changes
 ● political changes.

6 Would people at the time have regarded these changes as progress? Give reasons for your answer.

7 'The lives of all women changed immediately war broke out in 1914.' Do you agree with this statement? Support your answer with reasons and evidence from the sources.

3.9 Medicine in the First World War

In 1914 there were 18,000 hospital beds in the countries of the British Empire. During the war these countries had 2 million wounded troops to care for. In addition to this, 6 million troops fell ill with diseases caused by wartime conditions. To deal with this problem, governments had to increase the number of **doctors**, **nurses** and **hospitals**. By 1918 British troops were being treated by almost 150,000 doctors and nurses in 637,000 hospital beds.

The most common **wounds** were caused by bullets and shrapnel. This type of wound was not new, but surgeons learned a lot more about its treatment. **Gangrene** was common and doctors gradually became expert in treating it. In 1914, one in every 100 wounded soldiers developed **tetanus**. Scientists had been working for some time to find an antitoxin to kill the tetanus spores, and their work was given a boost. From 1915 all British soldiers were injected. As a result, only one in every 1000 wounded soldiers developed tetanus. Tetanus injections are common today.

Injections were also trialled to prevent **typhoid fever** in the trenches. They proved effective and are now used widely. There were no injections to prevent **typhus**, however, which had killed a million people in the Balkans by 1918.

Source A

In July 1914 Austria-Hungary attacked Serbia. A swift victory seemed likely. But during November typhus appeared in the Serbian army. The epidemic spread rapidly through trenches and troop trains. Over 150,000 people died in less than six months. The Austrians decided that they dare not advance into the area affected. The typhus germ held them up for six months. Who can say what the effect on the whole war would have been but for this delay?

From James Hemming, 'Mankind against the Killers', 1956.

First World War nurses at work with French casualties. The national importance of their work gave a boost to the status of nurses; and the increase in the number of nurses made it necessary to organize the profession. Registration of all qualified nurses started in 1919.

Source B

Surrounded by all those infected wounds and by men suffering and dying without our being able to help, I was consumed with a desire to discover something which would kill the infection.

Alexander Fleming, commenting on the experience of being a surgeon in the war. Ten years later, he discovered penicillin.

Source C

Source D

Surgery and war have always been interlinked. Surgery in peacetime is practised by a number of individuals all working at the same problems separately. In war, the surgeons of many nations come together to give men of their fighting forces the best possible treatment. To do this, they are all prepared to share their knowledge. They also get more help from others in wartime. Manufacturing firms will devote their resources to providing some drug or apparatus. Supplies, transport and equipment are all provided by governments. In wartime, surgeons are also spurred on to do much more work than they would have done in peacetime.

Adapted from Sir W. Heneage Ogilvie's introduction to a book on surgery published in 1953.

Source E

Marie and Pierre Curie in their laboratory, from a 1904 French magazine. X-rays had been discovered by Röntgen in 1895, and the Curies had studied their use. During the war Marie Curie worked for the French government. She pioneered the use of mobile X-ray units to provide pictures of shattered bones and the location of bullets and shrapnel. The war speeded up the medical use of X-rays throughout the world.

Wounds to the head and face accounted for 10 per cent of injuries. Surgeons got so much practice in treating them that many became specialists in plastic surgery after the war. **Blood transfusions** became a little more common, but only very slowly. Some doctors argued for blood banks but there was not the scientific or government support for the scheme. This limited doctors' success with bleeding stomach wounds.

There were also completely new forms of war wounds. There were 185,000 casualties with **gas burns** to the skin, throat and lungs. Doctors had no solutions for these burns; they could only reduce the pain. Yet there was one benefit: governments gave money to scientists to investigate **chemical warfare**. By chance, this research produced new drugs which have helped doctors. One example is emetine bismuth which can be used to treat **dysentery**.

'Shell shock' was also new. This was not an injury caused by explosions but a mental disorder affecting soldiers confined in the trenches under heavy bombardment. At times 10 per cent of all casualties had shell shock. Psychiatrists were called in to help. It was normally successfully treated. About 90 per cent of cases returned to combat. This treatment did a good deal to increase public acceptance of **psychiatry**.

The use of aircraft in the First World War made scientists think about the problems of breathing at altitude. **Liquid oxygen** was developed. As a spin-off, this was very helpful to surgeons. They used it for patients under anaesthetic.

Questions

Section A

1 Make a list of the changes which took place in medicine during the First World War.

2 Organize your list into types of change.

Section B

3 Why did so many changes happen?

4 What was more important to medical changes, the work of governments or the work of individuals?

3.10 War and the Arts

The First World War produced much vivid **poetry** which was written mainly by **soldier-poets**. The poems they wrote were based on their experiences in the war.

Rupert Brooke (1887–1915) volunteered for the army in 1914 and saw brief action in Belgium. He wrote five war sonnets, including '**The Soldier**' in December 1914. He died in April 1915 from blood poisoning on his way to the Dardanelles.

Siegfried Sassoon (1886–1967) fought at the Battle of the Somme and was awarded the Military Cross for bravery. He then became **disillusioned** with the war and openly criticized the generals and the government. He became bitter that the British newspapers did not tell the full truth about life and death in the trenches.

The war also produced many **paintings** which depicted battle scenes. Some paintings glorified the war. These were usually commissioned to show a particular regiment in heroic action. The Imperial War Museum employed a number of artists to record the war on canvas. Among them were two brothers, **Paul** and **John Nash**, who were both appalled by the loss of life. Their paintings reflected the grim reality of war. By 1917 art galleries were staging exhibitions which specialized in war paintings.

One important development taking place at this time was the art of making movie pictures (**cinematography**). At first, short newsreel clips were shown. Then, in 1916, a full-length feature film was made about the Battle of the Somme. Official cameramen recorded the build-up and the aftermath of the battle. Scenes of British soldiers unloading British-made shells before the battle were featured in the film. Gruesome images of dead German soldiers in their trenches were shown, but no pictures of dead British troops were included. The cameramen could not film the troops going 'over the top'. This was because the cameras were on huge tripods and could not be operated safely when the trenches were under fire. These scenes were 'staged' and filmed away from the actual battlefield. Lloyd-George wrote that the film showed what the men at the front were doing for the country and that their achievements were made possible by the sacrifices of people at home. The film made a huge impact and was watched by massive cinema audiences in Britain.

Source A

Now, God be thanked Who has matched us
   with His hour,
And caught our youth, and wakened us
   from sleeping.

From 'Peace' by Rupert Brooke, written in December 1914. This poem reflects the mood of patriotism and enthusiasm which greeted the outbreak of war.

Source B

The place was rotten with dead; green
   clumsy legs,
High booted, sprawled and grovelled along
   the saps;
And trunks face downward, in the sucking
   mud,
Wallowed like sand bags loosely filled;
And naked sodden buttocks, mats of hair,
Bulged, clotted heads slept in the
   plastering slime.
And then the rain began – the jolly old rain.

From 'Counter-Attack', by Siegfried Sassoon, published 1918. This poem describes the trenches.

Source C

The rain drives on, the stinking mud becomes more evilly yellow. The shell-holes fill up with green-white water; the black dying trees ooze and sweat, and the shells never cease. This land is one huge grave. It is unspeakable, godless, hopeless.

Paul Nash, the artist, speaking in 1917.

Source D

'Over the Top' by John Nash, painted in 1915.

Source E

Going 'over the top'. From the film 'Battle of the Somme', 1916.

Questions

1 How does the 'mood' of the poetry change between Source A and Source B? How can this be explained?

2 Which are more useful to an historian studying the First World War: war poems, war paintings or films of the war? Explain your answer.

3 'Films are bound to be more reliable than paintings as evidence of the war.' Do you agree or disagree with this statement? Give reasons for your answer.

4 Can art also be propaganda? Explain your answer.

4.1 Impact on Local Communities

The First World War had drastic effects. The **financial cost** to Britain was a staggering £9000 million. The government was forced to put up taxes and increase borrowing to meet the bill. Large areas of **countryside** in northern France and Belgium were destroyed by the fighting. Britain suffered little environmental damage but lost two-fifths of its **merchant shipping fleet**, sunk by the German U-boats.

Loss of life

The worst effect of the war was the terrible **loss of life.** On the first day of the Battle of the Somme, for example, 20,000 British troops were killed. People were left in a state of shock; no one had expected the war to result in so many dead and wounded. There was talk of a **lost generation** – those aged between 18 and 45 who had died. They included some of the country's most talented people.

The bodies of many of the soldiers were never recovered. At **Thiepval**, on the River Somme in France, a huge memorial was built after the war. It lists the names of 72,000 men who died at the Battle of the Somme and whose bodies were never found. Villages and towns all over Europe erected **war memorials** to commemorate their dead. All of this was a far cry from the patriotic enthusiasm which had greeted the outbreak of war in 1914.

_ Source A _____

The Thiepval Memorial erected in 1921, near Albert, in France.

_ Source B _____

In 1914 local communities sponsored the founding of locally based battalions to keep the companionship of peace during wartime. As reported in the Bradford *Daily Telegraph*, 'The special inducement is that young men shall serve shoulder to shoulder with their friends.' But men who served together could die together as well. The effect on a local community of a battle like the Somme was appalling. The Leeds Pals suffered more than 500 casualties on 1 July 1916. The Bradford *Daily Telegraph* printed double-page spreads of the local fallen men. They were still printing them well into August. It was obvious that a major tragedy had struck.

From Malcolm Brown, 'Tommy goes to War', 1978. Bradford raised two 'Pals Battalions'.

_ Source C _____

The war memorial at Itchen Abbas, a village in Hampshire, erected in March 1917. It records the names of seven men killed in action.

Source D

EASTON NEWS

THE GREAT SACRIFICE – The sad news has been received this week that Corporal Louis Collard, Grenadier Guards, was killed in action on 24 September. He was the second son of Mr and Mrs Charles Collard, of the Chestnut Horse Inn, Easton, to have made the great sacrifice. His elder brother, Corporal Patrick Collard, was killed in action in June. George, a third son, wrote home from the front to his parents, 'I am very sorry to say that Lou is dead. I heard it last night and I hardly need tell you it knocked me over.' This double sorrow is one in which all will sympathize with Mr and Mrs Collard, and if there's any consolation, it is in the fact that the body was found and buried with the honours accorded to a soldier who has died fighting for his king and country.

From the 'Hampshire Chronicle', 11 November 1916. Easton is a village in Hampshire.

Source E

HEAVY CASUALTIES IN BIG ADVANCE
LEEDS 'PALS' BATTALION LOSES MANY MEN

In the fighting last weekend, no battalion suffered more severely than the Leeds 'Pals'. Many more casualties are announced today as having occurred on 1 July, a day which will long be a fateful memory in Leeds. Yesterday, we announced the death of Captain E. C. Whitaker and Lieutenant S. Morris Bickersteth. Today we add the names of Captain S. T. A. Neil, Lieutenant J. G. Vause and Second Lieutenant T. Willey. Stanley T. A. Neil was the son of Mr W. W. Neil, assistant to the sewerage engineer of Leeds Corporation. He was 27 years of age and unmarried. Before the war he was resident engineer at New Leighton reservoir. When last home in Leeds he visited most of the homes of the Leeds Pals who had fallen.

From 'The Yorkshire Evening Post', 7 July 1916.

Source F

The Chestnut Horse Inn, Easton, today.

Questions

Section A

1 What were 'Pals Battalions'?

2 Why were memorials erected after the war?

3 How did the loss of life in the First World War affect:
   a family life?
   b town and village life?

Section B

4 Do Sources A and C tell us anything about people's attitudes at the end of the war? Explain your answer.

5 'Communities all over Britain suffered as a result of losing men in action during the war.' Use the evidence in this unit to test whether the statement is true or false and give your conclusion.

6 a Look at Sources A–F. Which one would be the most useful to an historian testing the statement in question 5? Explain your answer.
   b 'Source A is of no help in testing the statement in question 5. It is therefore useless to historians.' Do you agree? Explain your answer.
   c If some sources are not useful, does it mean that they will never be useful to a historian? Explain your answer.

7 Historians often talk about 'gaps' in their evidence.
   a What do you think they mean?
   b Can anything be done to fill the gaps? Explain your answer.

4.2 The Peace Treaties

At the end of the war **Woodrow Wilson**, the US President, drew up a list of **Fourteen Points**, which was his plan for a peaceful world. He wanted the peace agreement to be as fair as possible. The formation of the League of Nations was one of these points (see Unit 4.3). Another was the idea that all people should have the right to **self-determination** (that is, they should be able to choose the country they wanted to live in). The German government agreed to end the war in 1918 on the understanding that the peace agreement would be based on Wilson's Fourteen Points.

Between January and June 1919 a peace conference was held at the Palace of **Versailles**, near Paris. Much to their anger, the German **delegates** were not allowed to take part in any of the discussions. The talks were dominated by Georges **Clemenceau** of France, David **Lloyd George** of Britain, Vittorio **Orlando** of Italy and Woodrow **Wilson**. Clemenceau wanted to take revenge and make sure that Germany would never again be strong enough to attack France. Lloyd George had mixed feelings. He thought it would be wrong to punish Germany too harshly but he was also aware that many British people wanted to 'squeeze Germany until the pips squeaked'. Wilson was desperate that the talks should result in a peaceful world and he did not want to see Germany punished.

At the end of the conference a number of treaties were signed with the defeated countries. The one dealing with Germany was called the **Treaty of Versailles**. The Germans called this treaty a **diktat** – a dictated peace. Between them the treaties made many changes to Europe. But were they changes for the better?

Source A

PEACE AND FUTURE CANNON FODDER

The Tiger: "Curious! I seem to hear a child weeping!"

A cartoon published in Britain in 1919. It shows Lloyd George, Orlando, Clemenceau and Wilson. The child who will be an adult in 1940 has just seen the Treaty of Versailles.

Questions

Section A

1 What were the Fourteen Points?

2 What attitude did France, Britain and the USA have towards Germany at the start of the peace talks?

3 Why did the Germans call the treaty a 'diktat'?

4 a What attitude is shown towards Germany in Source A?
  b Why do you think this poster was produced?

Section B

5 What changes were made to Germany's boundaries by the Treaty of Versailles?

6 a What new countries were created as a result of the other treaties?
  b Who had ruled these areas in 1914?

7 List the other ways Germany changed in 1919 under the headings of:
  ● military changes
  ● political changes
  ● economic changes.
  In each case explain your choice.

8 Were these changes improvements? Give reasons and examples in your answer.

German losses

The Treaty of Versailles took a lot of valuable land from Germany. Alsace-Lorraine, for example, was rich in iron ore and coal which provided cheap raw materials for the German factories. As well as losing land, Germany also lost all its overseas **colonies** in Africa and Asia. These were to be helped towards **independence** by the League of Nations. Germany could no longer trade with these areas. Germany was made to say that it was **totally** to blame for starting the war. This was the famous **war-guilt** clause which was bitterly resented by the German people. Germany's air-force was to be abolished and its navy was limited to a few cruisers and destroyers. All German submarines were to be scrapped. The navy was cut to 15,000 and the army was not to be bigger than 100,000 men. **Conscription** (compulsory service) into the army was banned. Germany was ordered to pay war damages (**reparations**) of £6600 million – a staggering sum of money. Clemenceau thought that the treaty was not hard enough. Lloyd-George said it went too far and would only keep the peace for thirty years.

New countries

The other treaties broke up the **old empires** of Austria-Hungary, Russia and Turkey. Nine new countries were created from these empires. It proved very difficult, however, to put **self-determination** into practice. It was impossible to draw up boundaries so that everyone belonged to the country of their choice. Poland, for example, had not only Poles but also smaller groups of German-speaking and Russian-speaking people. The **League of Nations** was to look after the rights of such **minority** groups.

Changes made to Germany by the Treaty of Versailles, 1919.

Changes made to Central and Eastern Europe, 1919.

4.3 The League of Nations

The war had caused so much suffering that people were determined not to let it happen again. The US President Woodrow Wilson suggested that countries should join together and form a **League of Nations**. The aim of the League would be to stop future wars and to encourage countries to work together to make living conditions better. In 1919 the League seemed to point the way to a more peaceful world, but things did not go to plan.

Source A

A great number of people in Britain supported the League, remembering the horrors of the war. League of Nations Societies were founded in a number of towns. However, the Conservative government and the military chiefs were not so enthusiastic. The British had a vast empire to look after. Did they really want to step into every squabble in Europe and the rest of the world?

To the French, there was still only one enemy: Germany. If the League would help protect them from Germany, they were in favour of it. If not, they would have to make their own arrangements.

From Christopher Culpin, 'Making History', 1984.

The organization of League of Nations.

Headquarters based in Geneva, Switzerland

How the League was run ...

Assembly
Like a parliament. Had 42 member countries at the start, who met once a year to vote on important issues. Decisions had to be unanimous.

Council
Consisted of four permanent members who were joined by other countries in rotation. Met regularly to discuss serious problems; decisions taken by majority vote.

Secretariat
Carried out the administration of the League. Prepared reports for and kept records of the Assembly and Council.

Agencies of the League included ...

Permanent Court of Justice
Set up to settle legal disputes between countries.

International Labour Organization
Concerned with working conditions and social welfare issues.

High Commission for Refugees
Created to assist refugees throughout the world.

Weaknesses of the League

Many countries never joined the League, and this weakened its influence. The US Senate refused to join, and the Communist Soviet Union was kept out for political reasons. Many Asian countries, such as Japan, thought that the League was biased towards European countries. The League did not have its own army and was therefore like a toothless dog; it could 'bark' but could not make countries obey it.

Although the League was successful in settling some minor quarrels in the 1920s, it was totally ignored by more powerful countries in the 1930s. It failed to stop:

- Japan invading Manchuria (1931)
- Italy invading Abyssinia (1935)
- Germany taking territory in Europe (1936–9).

Why was it that such a good idea ended mainly in failure? The sources in this unit may help us to reach an answer. They illustrate the **attitudes** of the major countries towards the League.

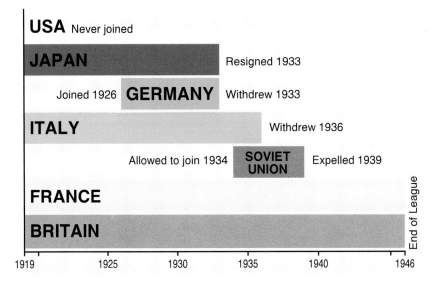

Membership of the League of Nations by the major countries, 1919–39. The League was disbanded in 1946.

Source B

> With peace, Wilson began to lose support. Americans felt that he should not have spent so much time at Versailles. They had entered the war to keep their country safe and had little sympathy in 1919 for their President's dream of a new world made safe from war. They were suspicious of the League of Nations because it might drag them into another war. So it was that the Senate refused to join it. In 1920 the new President, Warren Harding, said that the USA should not get caught up again in the quarrels of Europe.

From M. N. Duffy, 'The Twentieth Century', 1964.

Source C

A Democratic Party song sheet produced for the 1920 election. Wilson had been taken ill and James Cox was chosen by the Democrats to fight for the US presidency. Cox lost the presidential election to the Republican candidate Warren Harding.

Questions

Section A

1 Write a paragraph explaining how the League of Nations worked.

2 What were the main weaknesses of the League?

3 Give two examples of countries ignoring the League.

4 Study Source C. What message is it giving to voters in the USA?

Section B

5 At the end of 1918 most countries did not want another world war. Why, then, was the League not more fully supported by the countries of the world?

4.4 The Weimar Republic, 1919–29

At the end of the war Germany became a **democratic republic**. People were able to vote for the party of their choice. The first meeting of this new government took place in the town of Weimar and so it became known as the **Weimar Republic**. In June 1919 the Weimar politicians signed the Treaty of Versailles. Most German people resented the treaty, calling it a 'diktat'. There was deep anger that Germany had been made to accept the whole blame for starting the war. Within Germany, rumours spread that the German army could have fought on but it was forced to surrender by the politicians. There was a widespread feeling that the politicians had 'stabbed Germany in the back'.

This bitterness provided a breeding ground for **extreme** political parties. In 1919 the **Communists** tried, unsuccessfully, to overthrow the Weimar government. Then, in 1923, a revolt in Munich by the newly formed **National Socialist (Nazi) Party** had to be put down. The Nazi leader, **Adolf Hitler**, was sentenced to five years' imprisonment but he only served nine months. During this time he outlined his beliefs in a book called ***Mein Kampf*** (*'My Struggle'*). He described his hatred of the Treaty of Versailles and his desire to make Germany great again.

By 1923, the Weimar government was finding it impossible to keep up with the **reparations** it owed France. The French sent troops into the Ruhr with the intention of taking coal. The German government organized a campaign of **passive resistance**. The miners went on strike and refused to help the French. In order to pay the miners the German government printed huge amounts of money. This led to **hyper-inflation** in Germany. Money became worthless and prices soared. In November 1923 a loaf of bread cost 200,000 million marks!

Source A

By the death of Herr Stresemann, Germany has lost her ablest politician. Stresemann worked for the rebuilding of his shattered country. When he became Chancellor, Germany was in ruins. The French were in the Ruhr and the problem of reparations hung over a bankrupt Germany which was seething with unrest. He had extremists to the right and left to obstruct him at every turn. Germany is now orderly and prosperous and has a new standing in the affairs of Europe.

From 'The Times', 4 October 1929.

Political parties in Germany after 1918.

LEFT WING		CENTRE		RIGHT WING
COMMUNISTS	SOCIALIST PARTIES	CENTRE PARTY	NATIONALIST PARTY	NAZI PARTY
Wanted a Communist revolution in Germany similar to the one in Russia in 1917. They were against the Weimar Republic	Wanted the Weimar Republic to succeed. These parties were supported by most of the workers	Made up mainly of Catholics. It supported the Weimar Republic	Made up of landowners and factory owners. It hated the Weimar Republic and wanted the Kaiser to return	A Fascist party. Wanted a 'pure' German race and the abolition of the Treaty of Versailles. It, too, hated the Weimar Republic

In August 1923 **Gustav Stresemann** became the new **Chancellor** (Prime Minister) of Germany. He brought inflation to an end and called off the strikes in the Ruhr. In 1924, Stresemann signed the **Dawes Plan** with Britain, France and the USA. Under the Plan, Stresemann said that Germany would re-start paying reparations. The French agreed to leave the Ruhr and the Americans said they would lend money to help German industry.

In 1925, Stresemann signed the **Locarno Pact**. Under this he said that Germany would accept the terms of the Treaty of Versailles. Following this, in 1926, Germany was allowed to join the League of Nations.

Other countries were now beginning to view Germany in a more positive light. In Germany, prosperity was returning for many people. Then, on 3 October 1929, Stresemann died. Three weeks later the Wall Street crash took place and once again the Weimar government found itself facing problems.

Questions

Section A

1 Draw a timeline to show the main events between 1919 and 1929.

2 Describe the fortunes of Hitler and the Nazis in the 1920s.

Section B

3 **a** Explain the following words and phrases: **ditkat**, **'stab in the back'**, **passive resistance**, **hyper-inflation**.
b Are they connected in any way? Explain your answer.

4 Explain the views held by the various political parties in Germany after 1918.

5 How did people in the 1920s view the work of Gustav Stresemann? Explain your answer.

Source B

German cartoon of 1929. The nurse is saying, 'You're too late he (Stresemann) is dead.' The Nazis following Hugenberg are carrying manure, a stink bomb and placards saying 'Traitor' and 'Stresemann rot in hell'. Hugenberg was leader of the Nationalist Party.

5.1 Democracy under Threat, 1919–39

During the period 1919–39 many countries became **dictatorships** (ruled by one person – a **dictator**). This was especially true after the **Great Depression** of 1929–32 (see Unit 5.3), which brought worldwide mass unemployment and poverty. People demanded strong leadership to solve these problems. In countries where democracy was weak, dictators were able to seize power. Only in countries where democracy was firmly established, such as Britain, were dictators unable to gain a foothold.

Political ideas: Communism, Fascism and Democracy.

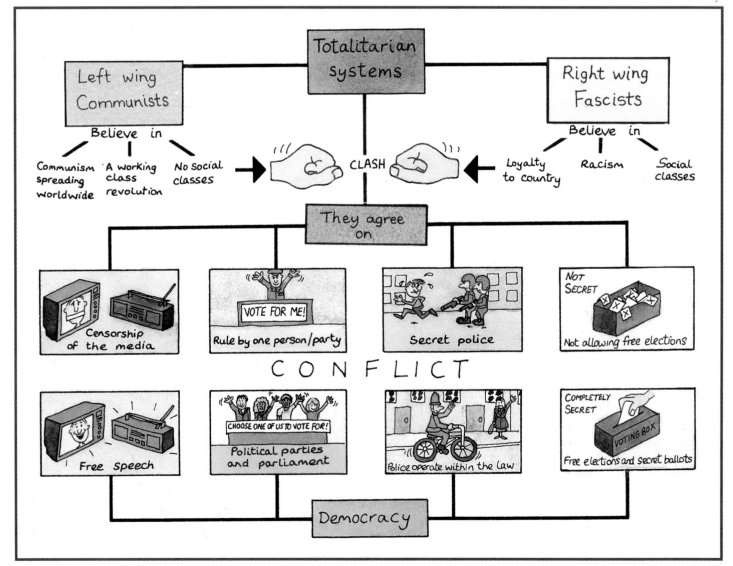

European Governments, 1919–39

Country	System of government, 1919–39
Spain	Democracy 1919–23; dictatorship 1923–31; democracy 1931–6; civil war 1936–9; dictatorship 1939
Portugal	Democracy 1919–28; dictatorship after 1928
Italy	Democracy 1919–22; dictatorship after 1922
Soviet Union	Communist dictatorship
Germany	Democracy 1919–33; dictatorship after 1933
Austria	Democracy 1919–32; dictatorship after 1932
Yugoslavia	Democracy 1919–29; dictatorship after 1929
Bulgaria	Democracy 1919–34; dictatorship after 1934
Hungary	Dictatorship
Poland	Democracy 1919–26; dictatorship after 1926
Estonia	Democracy 1919–34; dictatorship after 1934
Latvia	Democracy 1919–34; dictatorship after 1934
Lithuania	Democracy 1919–26; dictatorship after 1926
Romania	Democracy 1919–38; dictatorship after 1938
Greece	Democracy 1919–36; dictatorship after 1936

Britain, France, Belgium, Luxembourg, The Netherlands, Eire, Denmark, Sweden, Norway, Finland, Czechoslovakia and Switzerland were all democracies throughout the period.

Questions

Section A

1 Write a paragraph describing the difference between a **democracy** and a **dictatorship**.

2 Are Sources A and B examples of **propaganda**? Explain your answer.

Section B

3 a Design a table like the one below, listing each country or group of countries from the box above.

Country	System of government		
	1919	1930	1939
Britain France Spain			

b Use different colours to show democracy and dictatorship, based on information from the box above.

4 Write a paragraph to explain the changes shown by your table.

5 If a country changed from a democracy to a dictatorship it would be called a **political** change. Would this have led to **social** and **economic** changes in that country? Explain your answer.

6 'It was the world Depression of 1929–32 that brought about dictatorships in Europe.' Does your table lead you to agree or disagree with this statement? Explain your answer.

Source A

Ein Volk, ein Reich, ein Führer!

A Nazi poster from the 1930s. The slogan reads, 'One people, one state, one leader!'

Source B

A British anti-Fascist pamphlet, published in 1934.

5.2 Mussolini's Italy

In 1918 **Italy** was a very unsettled country. Many people were unhappy with the peace treaties. They believed that Italy should have been given more land as a reward for helping to win the war. There was also a lot of **unemployment** in the industrial north and terrible **poverty** in the agricultural south. Strikes and riots were common. Many landowners and factory owners were frightened that Italy would be taken over by the communists. The government was weak and did not seem able to do anything to make things better.

Enter Mussolini

In 1922 Benito Mussolini was the leader of the Italian **Fascist Party**. He told the Italians he would improve the country and make it great again like it had been in the days of the **Roman Empire**. In October 1922 Mussolini made a bid to gain power. Thirty thousand black-shirted Fascists (**blackshirts**) travelled to Rome and demanded to take control of the government (while Mussolini waited in Milan to see what happened). Rather than refusing the Fascists power, **King Victor Emmanuel III** sent a telegram to Mussolini inviting him to become the Prime Minister of Italy. The King was afraid that the Fascists would start a civil war if their demands were turned down. The Fascists had only intended the 'march on Rome' to be a show of power; they never really believed it would succeed.

Mussolini taking the salute at a military parade in Munich in 1937. Mussolini was keen for people to see photographs like this.

Once in power Mussolini set about removing the opposition. Groups of Fascist blackshirts went round beating up or murdering anyone who spoke out against Mussolini. By 1925, Mussolini had become the Fascist dictator of Italy, calling himself 'Il Duce' ('The Leader'). Mussolini was an ex-journalist, and he began a campaign of **propaganda** to win the acceptance of the people. Posters and photographs appeared showing him as a strong, confident leader who was making Italy a better country.

How successful was Mussolini? Did he live up to his word and improve living conditions in Italy?

A painting showing Mussolini with a group of blackshirts, by an Italian artist of the time.

Source C

The economic progress of Italy was the most successful aspect of Italian fascism. Hydro-electricity was used more fully, and attention was given to the improvement of road and rail transport. The Pontine Marshes near Rome were drained, and new towns were built on them. Mussolini gave increased help to the poverty-stricken south of Italy. The 'battle of the wheat' was a whole-hearted attempt to make Italy self-sufficient in wheat production.

From John Martell, 'The Twentieth Century World', 1969.

Source D

A lot of money was spent on public works: reclaiming land such as the Pontine Marshes outside Rome; building *autostrada* [main roads]; electrifying railways. Much of this was done for the sake of propaganda. Jobs were created but not in vast numbers. Unemployment rose during the 1930s. Wages stayed low, and Mussolini did little to help southern Italy, where many people continued to live in conditions of grinding poverty.

From Nicholas Tate, 'People and Events in the Modern World', 1989.

Source E

Out of 317 history textbooks which were in use in Italian schools, 101 were banned by Mussolini in 1926. By 1936 there was a single history textbook which was compulsory. The year 1922 was to be **anno primo** [the first year] of a new era in the history of Italy.

From C. C. Bayne-Jardine, 'Mussolini and Italy', 1966.

Source F

There is no doubt Mussolini did good for Italy. Towns became cleaner, public services improved, and the government became more efficient.

From Rupert Martin, 'Looking at Italy', 1966.

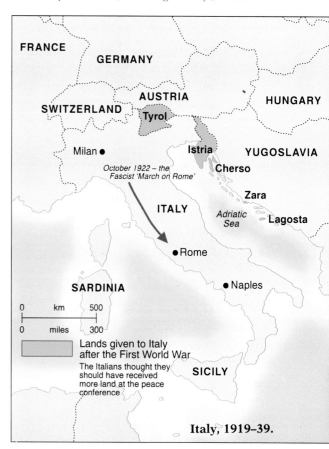

Italy, 1919–39.

Questions

Section A

1 What were conditions like in Italy in 1918?

2 Describe how Mussolini came to power.

3 Why was Mussolini keen for people to see him as he is shown in Source A?.

4 What impression does Source B give of the Fascists?

5 Source A is a photograph; Source B is a painting. Does this make Source A more reliable than Source B? Explain your answer.

Section B

6 Study Sources C and D.
   a In what ways do they differ?
   b Why do you think there are these differences?

7 Source F comes from a book which is mainly about the geography and culture of Italy. Source D was written by an historian. Does this mean that Source F is less accurate? Explain your answer.

8 Why do you think the changes in history textbooks were made (Source E)?

9 Historians often say that they try to give a balanced or **objective** view of events in the past. Is it possible to come to an objective view about Mussolini? Give reasons for your answer.

5.3 *The Great Depression*

The year 1929 was the year of the **Wall Street crash**. Prices on the US stock exchange, situated on Wall Street in New York, collapsed. As the USA had strong financial links with other countries (see diagram below), the world was plunged into an **economic depression** of falling trade, unemployment and poverty.

During the 1920s the USA had been very prosperous. Wages were high and it was easy to borrow money from the banks. There was a big **demand for industrial products** like motor cars, cookers and fridges. American industry was booming and share prices shot up to ridiculously high levels. Many Americans invested money in stocks and shares hoping to 'get rich quick'.

Then, on 24 October, it all went wrong. People sensed that the high share values were unrealistic. They began to **panic-sell** their shares and immediately the prices plummeted to nothing. People who had paid high prices for shares now found they were worthless. People became bankrupt overnight. As a result the demand for industrial products fell. Factories closed down and people were laid off. By 1932 there were 12 million people out of work in the USA.

Free trade and protection.

Source A

A British election poster of 1929.

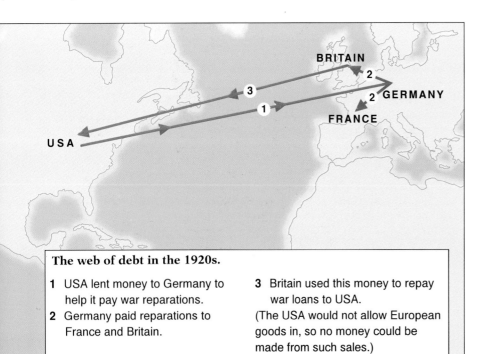

The web of debt in the 1920s.

1 USA lent money to Germany to help it pay war reparations.
2 Germany paid reparations to France and Britain.
3 Britain used this money to repay war loans to USA.
(The USA would not allow European goods in, so no money could be made from such sales.)

At first, the US government did very little to help the unemployed and millions were left living in poverty. The US government also stopped lending money to European countries.

After 1932, US President **Franklin D. Roosevelt** introduced policies to put people back to work, building dams and motorways. He also lent government money to farmers and industry. He called these measures the **New Deal**.

Britain did not enjoy the same prosperity as the USA in the 1920s. British industry had been losing trade since before 1914. More business was lost during the First World War when other countries, unable to obtain goods from Britain, started up their own factories. For most of the 1920s British industry, particularly coal-mining, shipbuilding and steel, was in a poor state. One factor which brought this about was the policy of **free trade**. Since 1860 Britain had allowed foreign goods to enter the country without charging any duty (customs tax). Other countries such as the USA, however, had a policy of **protection**. They charged duties on imported goods to make them more expensive than US products.

The Wall Street crash was the final nail in the economic coffin for Britain. World trade collapsed, British exports fell and more British factories were forced to close. By 1932 there were almost three million people out of work. The National Government (see Unit 5.7) was not very successful in coping with the Depression.

Germany also suffered from the Wall Street crash. The Depression caused six million people to lose their jobs. It also provided the chance for the Nazis to win power for the first time.

Questions

Section A

1 What is meant by **free trade** and **protection**?

2 What point is being made in Source A?

Section B

3 Why was Germany affected by the Wall Street crash? What were the effects for Germany?

4 a Copy cause-and-effect diagram 1 into your book. Fill in the boxes from the labels below (some have already been done for you):
  - Industry prosperous
  - Wall Street crash
  - High wages in USA
  - 12 million out of work
  - Factories close
  - People worried that things are 'too prosperous'
  - Big demand for goods
  - People buy shares
  - People sell shares quickly
  - Roosevelt's New Deal

  b Write a paragraph explaining the links in the diagram.

5 a Copy cause-and-effect diagram 2 into your book. Fill in the boxes from the labels below (some have already been done for you):
  - National Government in power, 1932
  - Coal-mining, shipbuilding and steel struggle in the 1920s
  - Free trade allows in cheap foreign goods
  - Wall Street crash
  - Countries start up own factories during First World War
  - Britain loses trade
  - USA stops lending money to Britain
  - Britain heavily involved in First World War
  - More factories close down
  - Three million out of work

  b Use colours to shade in boxes in your diagram which are **causes**, **effects** or **both**.

  c What were the long-term and short-term causes of the Depression in Britain?

  d 'The most important cause of the Depression in Britain was the Wall Street crash.' Do you agree? Give reasons for your answer.

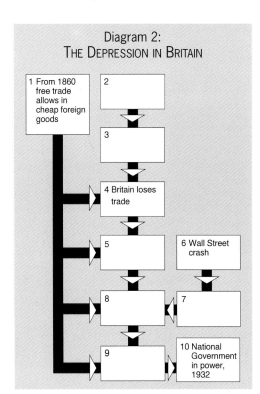

Diagram 1:
THE DEPRESSION IN THE USA

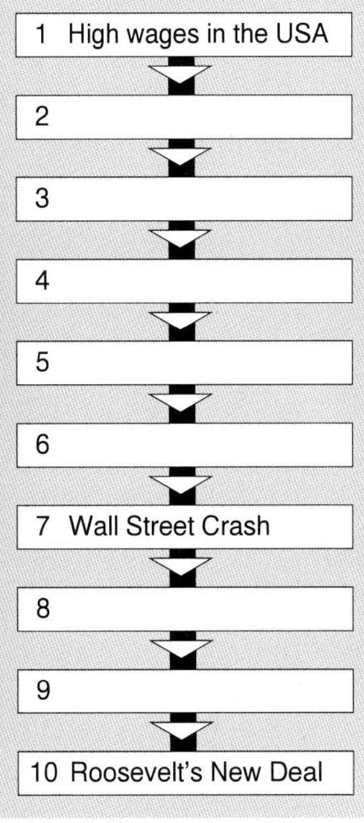

1 High wages in the USA
2
3
4
5
6
7 Wall Street Crash
8
9
10 Roosevelt's New Deal

Diagram 2:
THE DEPRESSION IN BRITAIN

1 From 1860 free trade allows in cheap foreign goods
2
3
4 Britain loses trade
5
6 Wall Street crash
8
7
9
10 National Government in power, 1932

5.4 Hitler Comes to Power

Between 1924 and 1929 the German **Nazi Party** was not very popular. These were relatively good years for Germany. On 3 October 1929 **Gustav Stresemann**, the successful German Chancellor, died. He had given his country back some pride following the troubled times of inflation. Then, on 24 October, the New York stock exchange on Wall Street crashed. The USA stopped lending money to Germany. In addition, like other countries, Germany was badly affected by the slump in world trade which followed. Factories were forced to close, and millions of people lost their jobs. This, it seemed, was a catastrophe without quick solutions.

Hitler campaigns for votes

In Germany, **Adolf Hitler** started to travel around the country making speeches. He said that a lot of Germany's problems were caused by the **Jews**. He promised that he would give the German people employment and rid the country of the Treaty of Versailles. Hitler was a brilliant speaker, and people listened closely to his message. His Nazi Party was well organized, producing posters, leaflets and books. The **SA**, or **brownshirts** – one of Hitler's private armies – broke up the meetings of the other political parties.

Source A

Hitler addressing a Nazi Party rally in 1933.

Source B

- We demand the joining together of all German people.
- We demand the abolition of the Treaty of Versailles.
- No Jew can be a citizen of Germany.
- We demand a strong government.
- There must be no more immigration of non-Germans into Germany.

From the Twenty-Five Points of the Nazi Party 1920.

Source C

'Our Last Hope – Hitler': a Nazi election poster of 1932.

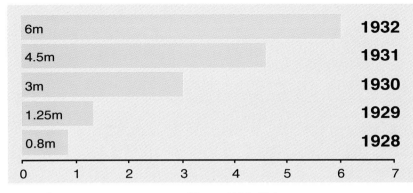

Unemployment in Germany, in millions, 1928–32.

Seats won in Reichstag elections 1928–33						
Party	Nazi	Nationalist	Communist	Centre Party	Socialists	Others
1928	12	60	54	78	153	134
1932 (Nov)	196	51	100	90	121	26
1933 (March)	288	52	81	92	120	14

Reichstag election results, 1928–33.

Many business people were afraid that the **Communists** would take over Germany. Hitler told them that if he got into power he would abolish the Communist Party. Business people gave huge amounts of money to Hitler to help him finance the Nazi Party.

The Nazis began to win more seats in the **Reichstag**, the German Parliament. By 1932 they were the single largest party. In January 1933 **President Hindenburg** appointed Hitler Chancellor of Germany. He thought Hitler would not last very long – but how wrong he was!

The Nazis did not have an **overall majority** in the Reichstag, and Hitler wanted to make his position safe. He decided to hold another election. Days before the election the Reichstag building was destroyed in a fire. Hitler blamed this on the Communists. The Nazis won even more seats and then joined forces, temporarily, with the **Nationalist Party** and the **Centre Party**. This gave Hitler the overall majority he wanted.

Führer of Germany

Hitler banned the Communist Party in 1933, using the Reichstag fire as an excuse. He then passed the **Enabling Act** which gave him the power to make laws without asking the consent of Parliament. In July 1933 he banned all political parties other than the Nazis. Finally, when President Hindenburg died in August 1934, Hitler made himself **Führer** (leader) of Germany. He was now the dictator of Germany.

Questions

Section A

1 Draw a timeline to cover the years 1919–34 in Germany. Show on it six events which you think were important in the rise of Hitler.

2 'The Nazi Party was well organized.' Which sources do you think support this statement? Explain your answer.

3 Is Source A reliable? Explain your answer.

Section B

4 Is there a connection between the diagram and the table above? Explain your answer.

5 Design a bar chart to show the results of the Reichstag elections between 1928 and 1933. Explain what it shows.

6 a Design a cause-and-effect diagram using these labels: Hitler made Chancellor 1933; the Nazis promise jobs; world Depression 1929–32; Nazis win most seats in the Reichstag.

  b Use different colours to shade in **causes** and **consequences**.

7 'Hitler was made Chancellor in 1933. This means that the Treaty of Versailles (1919) cannot have been one of the causes of his coming to power.' Do you agree? Give reasons for your answer.

8 Which of the following was most important in Hitler's coming to power: Hitler's ability as a speaker; the Nazis' Twenty-Five Points; the world Depression? Explain your answer.

9 What were the immediate results of Hitler being made Chancellor?

5.5 Life in Nazi Germany

Between 1919 and 1933 the people of Germany lived in a **democracy**. They were able to vote in elections for the party of their choice and could openly criticize the government. Workers could try to improve their wages and working conditions by joining a trade union. Young women were encouraged to follow a career, and many married mothers had jobs. People were free to marry whoever they liked. Schoolchildren studied a range of subjects and were free to decide whether they wanted to join a youth club.

There was little racism in Germany at this time. Jewish people were members of the professions. Many Jews were teachers, lawyers and doctors. How did all this **change** under the totalitarian rule of Hitler?

Once in power, Hitler set about taking complete control of German life. All political parties, except the Nazi Party, were banned. The laws were now made by Hitler. People had to obey or face punishment. Many who opposed Hitler were arrested by the **Gestapo** – the secret police – and sent to **concentration camps**.

Hitler wanted to turn Germany into a nation of 'pure' Germans. He claimed that the Jews were an inferior race of people and blamed them for the Depression. From April 1933 he told people not to buy goods from Jewish shops. He banned Jews from restaurants and cinemas: they had to be indoors before darkness fell. In 1935 he made it illegal for a non-Jewish German to marry a Jew.

The Nazis said that German **women** should have as many 'pure' children as possible – in this way German society would gradually rid itself of 'inferior' blood. German women were expected to stay at home and carry out their domestic duties.

The Nazis also told the **schools** what to teach. They realized that this was one of the best ways of instilling their political ideas. Jewish teachers and, eventually, Jewish students were expelled from the schools. The school curriculum became **biased** towards what the Nazis wanted the pupils to learn.

From 1936 it became compulsory for all German children to join the **Hitler Youth Movement**. Here boys and girls were taught Nazi beliefs outside of school hours. All other youth clubs were made illegal.

The Nazis banned any **art**, **literature** or **music** which did not fit in with their ideas. **Newspapers** could only print stories which were officially approved. Hitler used the 1936 **Berlin Olympic**

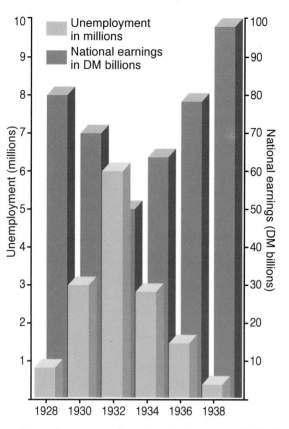

Unemployment and earnings in Germany, 1928–38.

Source A

A Nazi youth poster of 1933.

Games to glorify the Nazi Party. He was not pleased when a black (and therefore 'inferior') athlete from the USA named **Jesse Owens** won four gold medals. Each year the Nazis held a huge rally to demonstrate their power and strength.

In May 1933 Hitler banned **trade unions**. Instead, workers had to join the **German Labour Front.** This organization set out to bribe the workers by providing good facilities in the factories, such as canteens, and awarding paid holidays. Wages, however, hardly went up at all.

Source B

Periods	Monday	Tuesday	Wednesday	Thursday	Friday	Saturday
8:00–8:45	Deutsch	Deutsch	Deutsch	Deutsch	Deutsch	Deutsch
8:50–9:35	Geog.	History	Singing	Geog.	History	Singing
9:40–10:25	Race Study	Race Study	Race Study	Ideology	Ideology	Ideology
10:25–11:00	Recess, with sports and special announcements					
11:00–12:05	Domestic science with mathematics, every day					
12:10–12:55	Eugenics (Science lesson about 'breeding' pure Germans), Health Biology, alternating					

The timetable in a German girl's school after 1933.

Source C

A Nazi Party rally in Nuremburg in 1938.

Questions

Section A

1 a What does the diagram on page 72 suggest about life under the Nazis?

  b Would you trust this information? Explain your answer.

2 What message do you get from Source A?

3 a Compare Source B with your own school timetable. What similarities and differences are there?

  b Explain why there are these differences.

  c What do you think pupils in Nazi Germany would have been taught in their history lessons?

4 Why would Hitler have approved of Source C?

Section B

5 Use the sources and information in this unit to design a chart like the one below to trace **change** in Germany.

Aspect of life	1920s	Under Hitler

6 Did anything stay the same in Germany after 1933? Explain your answer.

7 Which of the changes do you think was the most important to the Nazis? Give reasons for your answer.

8 Would people in Germany have looked upon these changes as **progress**? Explain your answer.

Source D

It is probable that the number of people who disliked Nazism was very large. The number who openly protested was very small. The penalty was usually death. People who disliked, but did not resist, shut themselves off from what was happening. Resistance came from the churches, the Communists, some university students and some members of the upper classes.

From Alan White and Eric Hadley, 'Germany 1918–1949', 1990.

5.6 The Soviet Union in the 1930s

Industry	Production in millions of tonnes	
	1932	1938
Coal	64	132
Steel	12	32
Oil	22	32
Grain	38	60

Production figures for selected Soviet industries and farming, 1932 and 1938.

Lenin died in 1924. By 1927 **Joseph Stalin** had become dictator of the Communist **Soviet Union**. He announced his intention of 'dragging Russia into the 20th century', and introduced a succession of **five-year plans** to modernize heavy industry. Major industries such as coal-mining, steel and oil were set production targets over a period of five years. Small farms were joined together or **collectivized** to produce more grain. It was argued that larger, government-run collectives could share machinery, and that it was more efficient to farm big fields than small ones. Many of the richer middle-class peasants (**kulaks**) objected to losing their land.

Stalin was anxious to keep his position of total power. He started to root out anyone who he thought was against his methods. He was especially worried that many army generals were against him. With the help of the **NKVD** – the secret police – suspected '**enemies of the state**' were arrested and put on trial. Many people 'confessed' in court and were sent to labour camps; others were murdered or executed. These **purges** reached their height in 1937.

Stalin's methods have been the subject of much argument, and historians have different opinions about him. This unit looks at how some historians have **assessed** the rule of Stalin in the Soviet Union in the 1930s.

Source B

The poor peasants showed a wish to work together. In the late 1920s, when the first tractor factories were started, it became possible to give more money and machinery to farming.

After that not only poor but middle-class peasants joined the collective farms. By mid-1930, six million peasant farms were linked in collective farms, and in the summer of 1931 over 60 per cent of peasant families joined collective farms. Thanks to collectivization the last exploiting class – the kulaks – was eliminated.

From a Soviet textbook of 1982.

Source C

There were both good and bad points of Stalin's rule. We have read about the horrors of the purges, but can see that, though they cannot be excused, Stalin may have been worried about a take-over by the Red Army. By concentrating on heavy industry it could be claimed that Stalin laid the foundations of Russian strength which enabled the Soviet Union to defeat Germany in 1945.

From P. Mantin and C. Lankester, 'From Romanov to Gorbachev', 1989. This is an English textbook about Russian history.

Source A

A painting produced for the Soviet government of collective farm peasants holding a harvest supper, 1937.

Source D

A painting produced for the Soviet government in the 1930s. In the background is a newly completed hydroelectric dam.

Source E

Stalin, ignoring the great cost in human life and misery, claimed that collectivization was a success, for no more famines came to haunt the Russian people. The collective farms did grow more food than the tiny privately owned holdings had done; for example, 30–40 million tonnes of grain were produced every year. Now two million backward peasants learned to drive a tractor. New methods of farming were taught by 110,000 engineering and agricultural experts.

From E. Roberts, 'Stalin: Man of Steel', 1968. This is an English textbook.

Source F

The majority of the peasants confronted the government with desperate opposition. Collectivization became a cruel civil war. Rebellious villagers were surrounded by machine guns and forced to surrender. Masses of kulaks were deported to remote unpopulated lands in Siberia. Most peasants decided to give as little as possible of their property to the collective farms. They slaughtered their cattle, smashed implements and burned crops. Vast areas were left untilled. Famine stalked the towns.

From Isaac Deutscher, 'Stalin', 1949. Deutscher (1907–67) was born in Poland. He was expelled from the Polish Communist Party in the 1930s for criticizing Stalin. He came to live in England in 1939.

Questions

Section A

1 Write down definitions for the terms **collectivization** and **purges**.

2 How did Stalin justify the changes he made to industry and farming?

3 Why did Stalin carry out the purges?

4 What can be learned from Source A?

5 a Why do you think Sources A and D were produced?
  b Are these sources reliable? Give reasons for your answer.

Section B

6 Is Source B **fact** or **opinion**? Explain your answer.

7 a What are the differences between Sources B, E and F?
  b How can these differences be explained?

8 Of Sources B, C, E and F which would you say was the most **objective**? Give reasons for your answer.

5.7 Britain in the 1930s

Britain did not escape the effects of the **Wall Street crash**. By 1931 there was a serious slump in British industry, with 2.6 million people unemployed. **Ramsay MacDonald**'s Labour government was desperately short of money and applied to a group of bankers in the USA for a loan. The US bankers, however, were only willing to loan money if the British government reduced its spending, including cutting unemployment payments. Many Labour politicians would not agree to this, and MacDonald decided to resign as Prime Minister.

King George V, however, persuaded MacDonald to stay on at the head of a new **National Government** made up of Conservatives, Liberals and Labour politicians. Although most of the Labour Party opposed this, MacDonald agreed. At a general election in October 1931 the National Government won a huge majority. MacDonald said this would lead the country out of Depression.

Between 1932 and 1939 the National Government tried hard to do this. **Subsidies** to industry and the **taxing of foreign imports** were two of the measures they tried. Some people said the government should spend its way out of the Depression, by borrowing money and building new roads and factories – just as Hitler and Mussolini were doing. Among these was Oswald Mosley, soon to become leader of the small British Fascist Party. This advice was ignored. The National Government was only partly successful in curing the Depression. In the end, it was the outbreak of the Second World War which brought Britain back to full employment.

Source A

The 1930s were the best years of my life, working on a farm in Cambridgeshire. Nineteen thirty was a bad year, I seem to remember. We had to plough the potatoes back into the ground – nobody wanted them, we couldn't give them away. From 1936, however, life was splendid. Things were improved on the farm with the government paying us subsidies so that we could afford fertilizers.

The pace of life was much slower than now, and people seemed to get on better. Although I cannot remember the 'Jarrow Crusade', I do recall buying a radio in 1937. This provided excellent entertainment, with all the best bands having their concerts broadcasted. We also had an Austin Seven and often went to Yarmouth in the summer.

Source B

Front cover of an Ordnance Survey map from the 1930s.

Source C

A property advertisement from 1933.

Ernest Macer, a retired farmer, reminiscing in 1988.

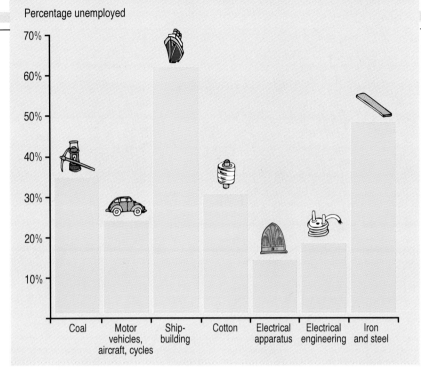

Percentage unemployed

Unemployment in Britain by industry in the early 1930s. The lighter electrical industries were located mainly in the south. Coal, steel and shipbuilding were mainly in the north.

Source D

Housing in the north-east of England in the 1930s.

Source E

Jarrow is dead. It is a derelict town. One out of two shops seems to be permanently closed. Wherever we went there were men hanging about, hundreds and thousands of them.

The writer J. B. Priestley describing Jarrow, Tyneside, in the 1930s. Priestley toured England and wrote down what he saw. Jarrow suffered from the closure of Palmer's Shipyard. In 1936, 200 men marched to London to ask Parliament to help. Their march was called the Jarrow Crusade.

Unemployment in some English towns and cities, 1934	
Town or city	Percentage of workforce unemployed
Jarrow	67.8
London	8.6
Merthyr	61.9
Luton	7.7
Gateshead	44.2
Watford	.7.0
Birmingham	6.4

Questions

Section A

1 Describe how the National Government came to power in 1931.

2 Name two things done by the National Government after 1931 to try to cure the Depression.

Section B

3 Source A is oral evidence. How reliable do you think it is? Give reasons for your answer.

4 The image in Source B was painted by an artist. What impression does it give of England in the 1930s?

5 Which are more useful to historians, statistics like those given in the diagram and the table above or eyewitness accounts such as Source E? Explain your answer.

6 Source C is an advertisement trying to get people to buy houses. Advertisements can be inaccurate. Does this mean that Source C is useless to historians?

7 Source D is a photograph. Does this make it more reliable than Source B? Give reasons for your answer.

8 Do the sources in this unit prove that life in the 1930s was better for people in the south of England than it was for people in the north?

6.1 Failure of the League of Nations (1)

During the 1930s the **League of Nations** was faced with three major problems. The fact that it did not solve them brought dire consequences.

Japan invades Manchuria, 1931

Japan became an industrial power in the late 19th century and set about building an empire. Soon Japan had a strong army and navy. The Japanese fought on the Allies' side in the **First World War** but were disappointed when they were not given any territory at the peace conference in 1919. The **Wall Street crash** brought high unemployment to Japan; its silk industry was badly hit. The Japanese government seemed unable to do anything about these problems. In 1931 the generals of the Japanese army decided to invade the Chinese province of **Manchuria**. The excuse used was that the Chinese had damaged a Japanese-run railway line. The generals had not consulted the Japanese government, but it soon realized that Manchuria's **coal** and **iron ore** would boost Japanese industry.

▆ Source A

A scene from an earlier war between Japan and China, in 1894–95. Japan won, gaining territory from China. Japan's thirst for an empire was fired by this war, which also showed its growing military strength.

Japan had controlled Port Arthur since 1905, Korea since 1910

Japan defeated China in a war in 1894–95

Japan had growing industries and wanted to take over territory. Manchuria was rich in raw materials and Japan could sell its products there.

Japanese occupation
By 1920s
1931–32

Map 1: Japan's growing power and the invasion of Manchuria, 1931.

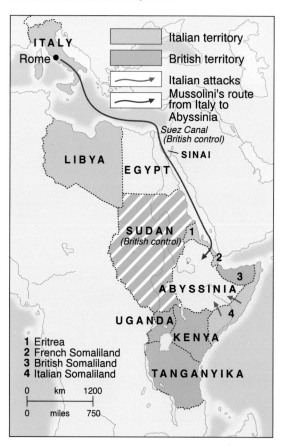

Italian territory
British territory
Italian attacks
Mussolini's route from Italy to Abyssinia

1 Eritrea
2 French Somaliland
3 British Somaliland
4 Italian Somaliland

Map 2: Italy's invasion of Abyssinia, 1935–36.

China asked the League of Nations to do something about Japan's aggression. The League sent a **commission of enquiry** to Manchuria to investigate. When the commission reported back in 1933 League members agreed that Japan was in the wrong. The League had no army to force Japan out, but it asked Japan to leave Manchuria. The Japanese ignored the request and resigned from the League. The League was shown to be powerless to control aggressive countries.

Disarmament

The **Treaty of Versailles** of 1919 had said that the League of Nations should get countries to **disarm** (destroy their weapons). It took until 1932 to set up a disarmament conference in Geneva. The problem was that although politicians agreed that disarmament was a good idea, no one was willing to make it happen in practice. There was too much distrust. Japan's actions in Manchuria did not help to increase confidence.

In 1933 **Hitler** decided to leave the talks and pulled Germany out of the League. He hated the Treaty of Versailles and wanted to destroy it. After this he started to **rearm** Germany. Now no one was interested in talking about getting rid of arms, and in 1934 the Geneva conference stopped meeting. Instead, countries began to build up their weapons to make themselves **secure** from attack.

Italy invades Abyssinia, 1935

Mussolini wanted **Italy** to have a big **empire** just like the Romans. This, he believed, would bring him personal glory. He was also anxious to take people's minds off the economic problems in Italy. Mussolini said that Italy had a right to territory in **Africa** and he sent a small number of troops into **Abyssinia** (modern Ethiopia) in 1934 to prepare for the main invasion force. Then, in October 1935 he attacked with the full might of the Italian air force and army. There was little the Abyssinian tribesmen could do in defence.

Haile Selassie, the Abyssinian Emperor, asked the League for help. The League applied **economic sanctions**; countries were told to stop trading with Italy, except in the vital item of **oil**. But the sanctions were not enough. **Britain** and **France** were too worried about the growing power of Hitler. They wanted to stay friendly with Mussolini so that he would side with them against Germany.

The message to other countries of this failure was clear: the League of Nations was weak and did not have the power to stop countries attacking others. Its failure as a peace-keeping body had been confirmed.

Questions

Section A

1 Copy out the following passage, choosing one of the words in *italics* each time.

Japan invaded Manchuria in *1931/1935*. The League said Japan was *right/wrong*. The League told Japan to *stay/withdraw*. Japan *stayed in/resigned from* the League.
In *1933/1934* the Geneva *rearmament/disarmament* conference *started/broke up*. Germany *joined/left* the League at about the same time.
In 1935 Italy invaded Abyssinia. *Mussolini/Hitler* ordered this invasion. The League told countries to *stop/start* trading with Italy. Mussolini *was frightened/took no notice* of the League. The League was shown to be a *success/failure*.

Section B

2 In Unit 5.3 you completed two cause-and-effect diagrams. Design two diagrams of your own to show:
   a the reasons why Japan invaded Manchuria.
   b the reasons why Italy invaded Abyssinia.

3 For each cause-and-effect diagram, shade in **causes**, **consequences** and events which were **both**.

4 Explain how the factors in your cause-and-effect diagrams link together.

5 'The event shown in Source A happened in 1894–95. This means it cannot have been one of the causes of Japan's invasion of Manchuria.' Do you agree or disagree? Give reasons for your answer.

6 This unit has described three problems which the League faced in the 1930s. Which of these problems do you think was the most important for the failure of the League? Give reasons for your answer.

7 Was the failure of the League of Nations **inevitable** (bound to happen)? Explain your answer.

6.2 Failure of the League of Nations (2)

The League of Nations was a popular subject for **cartoonists** during the 1920s and 1930s. One of the most famous cartoonists of the period was **David Low**, who worked for the London *Evening Standard*. Like other sources, cartoons have to be interpreted and evaluated before they can be used as historical evidence. Study the following cartoons, all drawn during the life of the League of Nations.

Source A

A cartoon from 'Punch' magazine, 1919.

Source B

'The Doormat': a cartoon by David Low, 1933.

Source C

'Barbarism' (top) and 'Civilization' (bottom): a cartoon by David Low, 1936. Here Low is commenting on events in Abyssinia.

Source D

A German cartoon of 1931 entitled, 'Wait a minute, I'm going to tell the League of Nations'.

Questions

1 Explain the point being made by each cartoon (Sources A–E).

2 Study Sources B and E. Explain the way Low has represented the League.

3 Which of these cartoons do you think is:
   a the most favourable to the League?
   b the least favourable to the League?
   Give reasons for your answers.

4 Are any of these cartoons **propaganda**? Explain your answer.

5 Do you think cartoons are more or less useful than newspapers for finding out about the actions of the League of Nations? Give reasons for your answer.

6 Cartoons often intend to amuse people or deliberately 'bend' the truth. Does this mean they are of no use to historians? Explain your answer, making close reference to the cartoons in this unit.

Source E

A cartoon by David Low, 1929. 'Peace' sits sadly on a donkey. By 1929 the disarmament conference, agreed in 1919, had still not been held.

6.3 The Spanish Civil War

For many years Spain had been controlled by the army, big landowners and the Catholic Church; these groups are often called the **traditional right**. Life was very hard for the poorer people. In 1931 King Alfonso XII **abdicated** after an election where the people voted for Spain to become a Republic. The new **Republican** government was **left wing**, made up of Socialists and Communists. It started to improve conditions for ordinary people. The traditional right wing and newly formed **Falange** (Fascist Party) did not like these changes. By 1936 Spain was in chaos. Churches were being burned down and strikes were breaking out all over the country. Many blamed the Republican government for not keeping order.

In 1936 **General Francisco Franco** led a **rebellion** of army generals against the Republican government which was based in Madrid. Franco was supported by the landowners, the Catholic Church and the Falange. The rebellion grew into a full-scale **civil war** to see who would control Spain. It lasted three years and cost the lives of 600,000 Spanish people.

Foreign involvement

The Fascists – or **Nationalists** – were helped by **Hitler** and **Mussolini** who both sent arms, troops and aeroplanes to attack the Republicans. Hitler and Mussolini saw the war as a chance to test out the efficiency of their weapons. The British and French governments said that the war was a matter for the Spanish to sort out and they did not intend to get involved. The **Soviet Union** sent weapons to help the Republicans.

In addition, the war captured the imagination of many individuals, who flocked to Spain to join in the fighting as volunteers. The Spanish Republican government formed **International Brigades** to recruit foreigners to fight on its side.

In April 1937 German bombers destroyed the small town of **Guernica** where the people supported the Republicans. The whole world was shocked by this event. The destructive effects of aerial bombing had been vividly shown. People realized that they could be the target of similar attacks in any future war involving their country. By January 1939 Franco's forces had won the war. Spain became a Fascist dictatorship.

Source A

A cartoon from 'Punch', November 1937. General Franco is shown as the 'face' of the smaller aeroplane; Mussolini is the larger one.

Source B

Spain became the arena where the forces of the Left did battle with those of the Right. People went from all over Europe to each side. Irish and English Catholics fought on the Nationalist side; Welsh coal-miners fought for the Republicans. When George Orwell was asked why he went to Spain he replied, 'This fascism, somebody's got to stop it.'

From W. O. Simpson, 'Changing Horizons: Britain 1914–80', 1986.

Source C

Here we are, soldiers of a revolutionary army, defending democracy against fascism.

Comment by George Orwell, the novelist, who went to Spain to fight on the Republican side.

Source D

'Guernica', painted by the great Spanish artist Pablo Picasso in 1938.

Source E

> Freedom is an easily spoken word
> But facts are stubborn things. Here, too, in Spain
> Our fight's not won till the workers of all the world
> Stand by our guard on Huesca's Plain
> Swear that our dead fought not in vain,
> Raise the red flag triumphantly
> For Communism and liberty.

The last verse of a poem entitled 'Full Moon at Tirez: Before the Storming of Huesca', written by John Cornford in 1936. He fought on the Republican side and was killed in action in 1936.

Source F

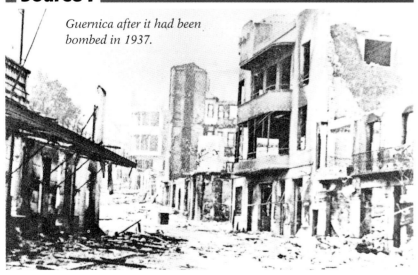

Guernica after it had been bombed in 1937.

Questions

Section A

1 List the following groups in Spain under the headings of **right wing** and **left wing**: Nationalists; Communists; Catholic Church; Republicans; Army; Fascists; Socialists; Large landowners.

2 Why did a civil war start in Spain in 1936?

3 What were the results of the war?

Section B

4 What viewpoints are shown about the Spanish Civil War in Sources A and D? Explain your answer.

5 Explain the reactions of the governments of France, Britain, Germany, Italy and the Soviet Union to events in Spain.

6 Why did many people 'flock to Spain' to fight in the war?

7 The bombing of Guernica (Source F) was shown on cinema newsreels in countries outside Spain. How might people have reacted to it? Explain your answer.

6.4 Five Steps to War

Step 1: German rearmament

The Depression of 1929–32 increased the support for extremist parties in Germany. As a result, in 1933, Hitler came to power. Hitler took Germany out of the League of Nations and started to **rearm**. In 1935 he introduced **conscription** and started to build up Germany's armed forces. In 1935 Britain signed an agreement with Hitler which said that Germany could build a navy up to one third of the size of Britain's.

Step 2: Remilitarization of the Rhineland

In March 1936 Hitler sent German troops back into the **Rhineland** – the 1919 Treaty of Versailles had banned them from this area. Hitler's generals had orders to withdraw if they were challenged – but no one did challenge them. There were mild protests from Britain; but many argued that the Rhineland was German territory and Hitler could do what he liked with it. Even the French were not motivated to take action. The League of Nations was trying to deal with Italy's invasion of Abyssinia and was powerless to stop Hitler. The League was fast showing itself to be totally ineffective.

Source A

During the 1930s both Britain and France were keen to avoid war. Memories of the First World War were still fresh and many thought the Germans were the unfair victims of Versailles. Appeasement seemed to make sense for Britain, which was suffering from the Depression and whose armed forces needed strengthening. For his part Hitler was confident Britain and France would not help Poland.

From Nigel Kelly, 'The Second World War', 1989.

Source B

Hitler made his aims clear in *Mein Kampf*. He intended to unite all German-speaking peoples and to build an empire. This foreign territory, which he called *Lebensraum* – living space – would probably be in eastern Europe. It would be wrong to think that Hitler had a detailed master-plan to take over Europe. Events did go his way in 1936–39, but they were not planned. He was helped by France's weakness and Britain's reluctance to consider war. It would also be wrong to think of Hitler as a power-crazed maniac; he showed great care and skill in using the opportunities which came his way.

From Christopher Culpin, 'Making History', 1984.

The five steps to war.

84

Step 3: The Anschluss

Hitler made no more demands for two years. He did, however, send his forces to help Franco in the **Spanish Civil War**. Then, in March 1938 he demanded that **Austria** should be joined with Germany in an *Anschluss* or union. Austria, Hitler said, was German speaking and so should become part of a 'Greater Germany'. German troops marched into Austria unchallenged.

Step 4: The Sudetenland and Czechoslovakia

In the summer of 1938 Hitler said that the **Sudetenland**, a German-speaking area of Czechoslovakia, should also be joined to Germany. Because of an agreement made in the 1920s, Britain and France were pledged to defend Czechoslovakia if it objected. The British began to prepare for war. People began to dig air-raid shelters and gas-masks were given out.

Some British politicians argued that force should be used to stop Hitler. Others, like **Neville Chamberlain**, the Prime Minister, favoured **appeasement** (see Unit 6.5). He believed that if Hitler was given this territory he would be satisfied and would make no more demands. On 30 September 1938 Chamberlain signed the **Munich Agreement** with Hitler, giving Germany the Sudetenland. The Czechs were not allowed any say in the matter. Chamberlain said it was 'peace with honour'.

In March 1939 Hitler invaded the rest of **Czechoslovakia**. This invasion broke the Munich Agreement. Chamberlain realized that his policy had failed. Britain speeded up its rearmament programme and the government called up men between the ages of twenty and twenty one for military training.

Step 5: Poland

In August 1939 the **Nazi–Soviet Non-Aggression Pact** was announced. Germany and the Soviet Union agreed not to go to war and to split Poland between them. (Poland had gained land from Germany and Russia under the Treaty of Versailles.) Hitler invaded Poland on 1 September 1939. Britain and France asked him to withdraw or they would declare war. Hitler ignored this request. On 3 September 1939 Britain declared war on Germany.

Step 1	Germany started to *rearm*, 1934–5
Step 2	Hitler sent troops into the Rhineland, 1936
Step 3	Hitler joined Austria to Germany (the *Anschluss*), March 1938
Step 4	Hitler took the Sudetenland, October 1938, and the rest of Czechoslovakia, March 1939
Step 5	Hitler invaded Poland, 1 September 1939

Source C

The 48 hours after the march into the Rhineland were the most nerve-racking in my life. If the French had marched into the Rhineland we would have had to withdraw, for the military resources at our disposal would have been wholly inadequate for even a moderate resistance.

Adolf Hitler speaking in the late 1930s.

Questions

Section A

1 Draw a timeline of the main events from 1929 to 1939.

2 What examples are there in the text of Hitler breaking the terms of the Treaty of Versailles?

Section B

3 Explain how the following factors might have been causes of the Second World War:
- the Treaty of Versailles
- the Depression
- Hitler's coming to power
- the Munich Agreement
- the Nazi–Soviet Pact.

4 Give one **long-term** and one **short-term** cause of the war and explain your choice.

5 Draw a cause-and-effect diagram showing the causes of the war and how they were linked together.

6 Both the League of Nations and Britain might have stopped Hitler taking territory. Why didn't they?

7 'Hitler and Hitler alone caused the Second World War.' Do you agree or disagree with this statement? Give reasons for your answer.

6.5
Neville Chamberlain and Appeasement

In 1938 the British Prime Minister **Neville Chamberlain** used a policy of **appeasement** when Hitler demanded the **Sudetenland** from **Czechoslovakia**. Chamberlain felt that if Hitler was given the Sudetenland he would make no more aggressive moves. Chamberlain had been horrified by the First World War and believed that another war would destroy Europe. He flew to talk with Hitler on three occasions, and on 30 September 1938 in Munich the two men reached an agreement. Chamberlain agreed to give the Sudetenland to Germany in the belief that Hitler would take no more territory.

At first Chamberlain was considered a national hero, because he had avoided war with Germany. Within six months, however, Hitler had broken the Munich Agreement and taken the rest of Czechoslovakia. From this time on, war became more and more likely.

When Britain did declare war on 3 September 1939, Chamberlain was a broken man. He believed he had done his best to avoid war. Now, however, people's opinion of Chamberlain changed. They argued that war occurred because Britain had given in to Hitler in 1938. In May 1940 Chamberlain was replaced as Prime Minister by **Winston Churchill**.

Historians have ridiculed Chamberlain, saying he was weak. But more recently there have been attempts to clear his name.

Source A

Chamberlain could not face the idea of war. Yet it could not have been plainer that, unless a firm stand were made against Hitler, even at the cost of fighting, all Europe would become controlled by the Nazis. This was a truth which Chamberlain refused to admit. Completely unwarlike in temperament, he was ready to make any sacrifice to avoid a conflict. Chamberlain flew back to London waving a scrap of paper bearing Hitler's autograph. He even called it 'peace with honour'.

From Malcolm Thomson, 'The Life and Times of Winston Churchill', 1945. Churchill was still alive at the time this biography was published. The book describes Churchill as 'the greatest national leader in British history'.

Source B

We, the German Führer and Chancellor and the British Prime Minister, have had a further meeting today and are agreed in recognising that the question of Anglo-German relations is of the first importance for the two countries and for Europe.

We regard the agreement signed last night and the Anglo-German Naval Agreement as symbolic of the desire of our two peoples never to go to war with one another again.

We are resolved that the method of consultation shall be the method adopted to deal with any other questions that may concern our two countries, and we are determined to continue our efforts to remove possible sources of difference and thus to contribute to assure the peace of Europe.

September 30. 1938.

The 'scrap of paper' signed by Chamberlain and Hitler on 30 September 1938.

Source C

If our leaders had been sufficiently educated to have read *Mein Kampf* they would have known it all. But it took Hitler's breach of his word to him, Neville Chamberlain, and the swallowing up of Czechoslovakia to open his eyes. On 3 September 1939 Chamberlain broadcast to the nation. Many of us remember the uninspiring speech about himself, 'Everything I have worked for has crashed into ruins' – as if that were the most regrettable aspect of the matter.

From A. L. Rowse, 'The Churchills', 1966. This book tells the story of the Churchill family.

Chamberlain had three meetings with Hitler about the Sudetenland.

1 At Berchtesgaden, 15 September 1938

2 At Godesberg, 22 September 1938

3 At Munich, 28–30 September 1938
He returned claiming he had brought back 'Peace in our time'.

The Sudetenland in Czechoslovakia. This area had three million German-speaking people. It was also an industrial area.

The Munich crisis, 1938.

Source F

A cartoon entitled, 'A Great Mediator', from October 1938. Chamberlain is on the left.

Questions

Section A

1 What does **appeasement** mean?

2 Write a paragraph describing Chamberlain's talks with Hitler in 1938.

3 What does Source F suggest about people's attitude to Chamberlain in 1938?

4 What happened after the Munich Agreement?

Section B

5 Study Sources C and D. Are they fact or opinion? Explain your answer.

6 What differences in views are given in Sources A and C–E about Neville Chamberlain?

7 These sources deal with the same events. Why, then, do they differ?

8 Which of the viewpoints here do you think is the most accurate? Explain your answer.

9 Do you think it will ever be possible for historians to decide **definitely** whether Chamberlain's policy was right or wrong? Give reasons for your answer.

Source D

There had been nothing weak or foolish about the attitude of Chamberlain. He had tried to settle differences by discussion and conciliation, methods which had been highly successful in the 1920s. Their failure was due to the fact that Hitler took conciliation for weakness and found that he could get his way. He could have been stopped earlier but only at the risk of a war. Discussion was the method of honourable gentlemen, which explains why Chamberlain favoured it and why Hitler did not.

From W. Robson, 'Twentieth-Century Britain', 1973. This is a school textbook.

Source E

Chamberlain had feared that history might judge him harshly, and he was correct. The opening of new records explains his policy. Chamberlain's reputation stands better now than it has ever done. The venom of his opponents pursued him long, but his was the only policy which offered any hope of avoiding war – and of saving lives and the British Empire.

From John Charmley, 'Chamberlain and the Lost Peace', 1989. This historian used new evidence based on Chamberlain's private papers.

7.1 The Rise and Fall of the Axis

The **war in Europe** passed through **three main phases**. The first saw Hitler's forces sweep through Europe with almost unbroken success. This lasted until towards the end of 1942. By this time Hitler controlled territory stretching from the Atlantic coast in the west to almost 1000 kilometres inside Russia. The second phase witnessed major defeats for the German forces and the halting of their advance. Finally, from about the beginning of 1943, the Allies gradually pushed the Germans back until they surrendered in May 1945.

When Hitler invaded Poland in September 1939, Poland was quickly defeated. So little happened during the next few months that the conflict became known as the '**phoney war**'. Then, in the spring of 1940, Hitler launched his **Blitzkrieg** (lightning war) in the west. Denmark, Norway, the Netherlands and Belgium all fell in quick succession. France followed soon after.

Britain found itself facing Germany alone. The USA was not yet involved, and the Soviet Union had signed a non-aggression pact with Hitler before the war. However, Hitler's plans to invade Britain had to be abandoned when he failed to gain control of the skies during the **Battle of Britain** in the summer of 1940.

Hitler turned his attention to the Soviet Union. On 22 June 1941 he launched a massive invasion, breaking the Nazi-Soviet Pact. The Germans advanced deep into Russian territory, until they were held up at **Stalingrad** in the winter of 1942. By this time Britain and the Soviet Union had gained another ally. When the Japanese

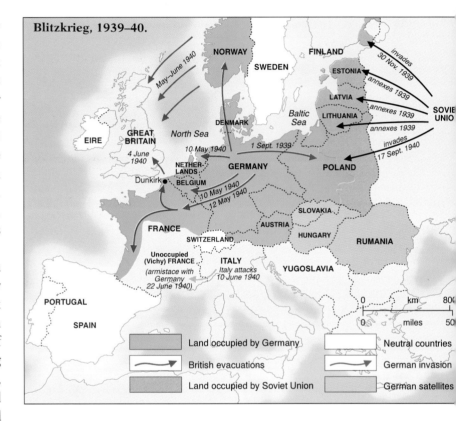

Blitzkrieg, 1939–40.

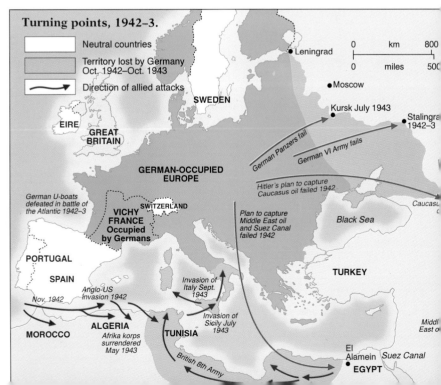

Turning points, 1942–3.

attacked **Pearl Harbor** in December 1941 the other **Axis** powers declared war on the USA.

The success of the Axis (Germany, Italy, Japan and their lesser allies) reached its peak in the winter of 1942. From then on the **Allies** achieved notable victories.

Montgomery's defeat of Rommel at **El Alamein** in October 1942 allowed the British to advance 1600 kilometres through North Africa. With the landing of US troops in Morocco, Axis forces were pushed out of North Africa. Allied forces advanced through Italy in 1943 and 1944.

Meanwhile the German defeat at Stalingrad was followed by their steady retreat back to Germany from the east. The net was closing in. On 6 June 1944 – D-Day – the Allies landed in France. Surrounded on all fronts, Germany surrendered on 8 May 1945.

Source A

Until the Japanese attacked Pearl Harbor, the United States naval base in Hawaii, on 7 December 1941, the war remained essentially a European war. Until December 1941 the battlefield was exclusively European and Atlantic; thereafter it became also Asiatic and Pacific.

From David Thomson, 'Europe since Napoleon', 1966.

Questions

Section A

1 Which were the main Axis powers during the Second World War?

2 Which countries fought on the Allied side during the Second World War?

3 Draw a timeline to show the important events during the war in Europe from 1939 to 1945. Use the maps to help you.

Section B

4 How did the fortunes of the Axis powers change during the course of the war?

5 What were the turning points which changed the course of the war? Give reasons for your answer.

6 a How did the war change after the Japanese attacked Pearl Harbour, according to Source A?

b In what way did it stay the same?

c List the changes affecting the fortunes of the Axis and those affecting where the war was fought.

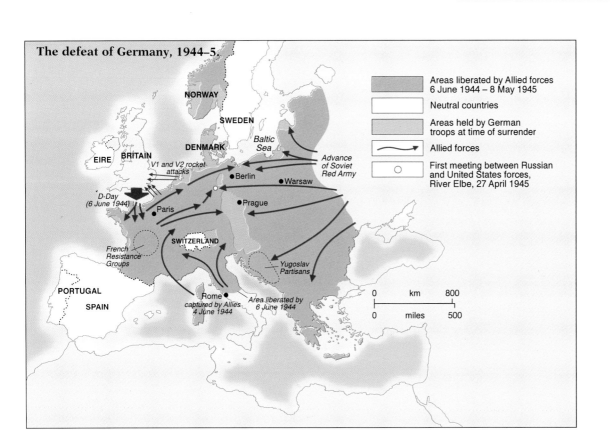

The defeat of Germany, 1944–5.

7.2 The War in the East

On 7 December 1941, **Japan** launched an attack on the US naval base at **Pearl Harbor**, Hawaii. Similar attacks on US and British bases in the **Pacific** followed. By March 1942 Guam, Wake Island and the Philippines had been lost by the USA. The British were forced to surrender Hong Kong and Singapore to the Japanese, who also invaded Burma and Malaya. Australia was threatened by the fall of the Dutch East Indies and most of New Guinea.

The USA had been caught by surprise. But as soon as the country was organized for war it was able to fight back with devastating effect. American naval successes were won with the **Battle of the Coral Sea** in May and at **Midway Island** in June 1942. Under the leadership of **General MacArthur**, the USA began to win back vital islands. This 'island hopping' brought Japan itself within striking distance. Meanwhile British troops were involved in a difficult campaign to free Burma and open up the '**Burma road**' to China.

The Americans continued their advance through the Pacific. In October 1944 they won a vital victory at **Leyte Gulf**. The Philippines were won back in January 1945, and the islands of Iwo Jima and Okinawa in February and May. From these bases the US could bomb Japan itself.

Japan appeared exhausted but refused to surrender. The decision was taken to drop **atomic bombs** on Japan in August 1945 (see Unit 7.5). The Japanese surrender was signed on the USS *Missouri* on 2 September 1945.

Why did Japan invade Pearl Harbor?

Looking back, it seems strange that Japan attacked the USA in the first place. After all, it was taking on the world's most powerful nation. To understand the decision it is necessary to study the Japanese in the 1920s and 1930s.

The Japanese had little time for politicians. There was much more respect for generals and admirals. Compared with politicians they appeared honourable and loyal to their country. These military leaders were gaining increasing power inside Japan. They wanted to make Japan a world power. They were frustrated by an agreement of 1923 which kept Japan's navy smaller than either Britain's or that of the USA. Japan had few natural resources to become a modern industrialized nation. They needed to get supplies like rubber,

Source A

US troops set up a victory flag on the island of Iwo Jima in the Pacific, 1945.

Source B

Of the eight US battleships, the *Arizona*, *Oklahoma*, *West Virginia* and *California* were sunk, and the *Maryland*, *Nevada*, *Pennsylvania* and *Tennessee* were severely damaged. Sunk, too, were three destroyers and four smaller vessels, while three light cruisers and a seaplane tender were badly damaged. Of US aircraft, 188 were destroyed, and 63 damaged. Of human casualties, the Americans had 3435 killed or wounded.

Details of US losses at Pearl Harbor. From Basil Liddell Hart, 'History of the Second World War', 1970.

metals and oil from elsewhere. Meanwhile the population was increasing rapidly. During the world depression there was widespread unemployment and a real fear of mass starvation. Japan's military leaders decided to make a bid for power.

In 1931 the Japanese overran **Manchuria** on the Chinese mainland; in 1937 the rest of China was invaded. Islands in the Pacific were taken over. These provided Japan with much needed raw materials, but brought Japan into conflict with Britain and the USA who also had interests in South-East Asia and the Pacific. Australia, too, felt threatened by the Japanese advance. Encouraged by Hitler's success in Europe the Japanese made plans to extend their empire in Asia.

Japan relied on buying its oil from the USA. In 1941 the US government refused to sell any more oil to Japan. Japan was desperate; they could not survive without oil. The Dutch East Indies had plenty of oil, but an attack here would be resisted by Britain and the USA. If the US fleet were destroyed in a sudden unexpected attack, Japan would have time to take over the rest of South-East Asia and the Pacific. The Americans would have no means to stop it. The British army would be no match for the Japanese and the native people of Asia would prefer the rule of fellow Asians to that of Western imperialists.

Although great damage was done to the US fleet at Pearl Harbor the Japanese plan failed. The aircraft carriers were at sea and so escaped destruction. The US navy was able to recover and counter-attack. Japan had 'aroused a sleeping giant'.

Source C

An American poster produced in 1945.

Questions

Section A

1 Draw a timeline to show the main events in the war in the East from 1941 to 1945. Use the map to help you.

2 Do you think the poster in Source C was produced before or after the victory at Iwo Jima? Give reasons for your answer.

3 Does Source B provide evidence that Japan's attack on Pearl Harbor was a success?

Section B

4 Consider the reasons for the Japanese attack on Pearl Harbor.
   a Did the Japanese attack for more than one reason? Explain your answer.
   b Arrange the reasons for the attack under the following headings: **political reasons**; **economic reasons**; **military reasons**.
   c Explain the links between the different types of reasons.
   d 'Japan needed time to build an empire in the Pacific to relieve the pressure of population increase at home.' Do you agree that this was the most important reason for the decision to attack Pearl Harbor? Give reasons for your answer.

5 What were the short-term and long-term **consequences** of the Japanese attack on Pearl Harbor?

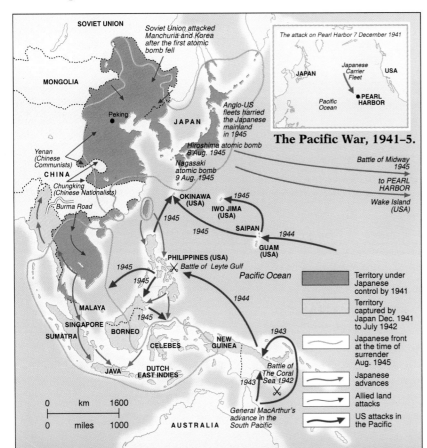

The Pacific War, 1941–5.

7.3 'Operation Barbarossa'

On 22 June 1941 **Hitler** launched his invasion of the **Soviet Union**. Despite the Nazi-Soviet Non-Aggression Pact, agreed with **Stalin** in 1939, Hitler had always intended to conquer the Soviet Union. He hated communism and wished to destroy it. He believed the Slavic people to be an inferior race, and that land taken from the Slavs would provide *Lebensraum* (living space) for the German 'master race'. The Soviet Union would provide Germany with vital raw materials. Furthermore, with the Soviet Union defeated, Hitler would control the European continent – no country could oppose him.

Germany's invasion plan was codenamed **Operation Barbarossa**. At first the invasion went well. Three armies cut deep into Soviet territory. Their targets were **Leningrad** in the north. **Moscow** in the centre and **Stalingrad** and the **Caucasus oilfields** in the south. By the winter of 1941 they had advanced almost 650 kilometres and were laying siege to Leningrad and Moscow.

But the advance stopped there. The Red Army had carried out a **scorched earth policy**. Everything which could be of any use to the German armies was either destroyed or transferred to safety beyond the Ural Mountains. The Soviet troops were able to hold their lines, and the Germans were on the defensive during the winter of 1941–2.

In the spring of 1942, Hitler ordered his forces to concentrate on a push in the south. The aim was to gain control of the oilfields in the Caucasus. By August 1942 German forces had advanced as far as **Stalingrad**. The battle which followed was one of the bloodiest and most important of the war. Despite terrible losses, the Soviet forces fought for every inch of the city which bore the name of their leader. The German Sixth Army under **General von Paulus** asked for permission to retreat and regroup at the onset of winter. Hitler refused. Cold, hungry and cut off from their supply lines, the Sixth Army surrendered in February 1943.

This proved that the German army could be beaten. Not only was the advance held up, but the Red Army was in a position to counter-attack. Soviet troops regained 480,000 square kilometres of land in the early months of 1943. That July they won an important tank battle at **Kursk**. The Germans were now in retreat.

Source A

The German armed forces must be prepared, even before the conclusion of the war against Britain, to crush Soviet Russia in a rapid campaign. I shall issue orders for the deployment against Soviet Russia eight weeks before the operation is timed to begin. Preparations which require more time than this will be put in hand now and will be concluded by 15 May 1941. It is of vital importance that our intention to attack should not be known.

Hitler's secret directive to the German forces, dated 18 December 1940.

Source B

Then the winter weather halted the German armies, unprepared for the terrible conditions. Tank crews had to keep fires burning beneath the engines of tanks to stop them freezing completely. The Germans had been issued with boots that fitted them exactly and so they could not wear more than one pair of socks. Thousands suffered from frostbite and thousands suffered hunger as the supply trucks slithered to a halt.

From C. C. Bayne Jardine, 'World War Two', 1968.

Source C

YIELD NOT AN INCH !

WASTE NOT A MINUTE !

A British poster aimed at encouraging co-operation between British workers and Soviet soldiers, 1944.

Source D

ОТСТОИМ
ВОЛГУ-МАТУШКУ!

Hitler's greatest mistake

Hitler's plan had been a spectacular failure. Before 'Operation Barbarossa', only Britain had stood against him, unable to do much to halt the German war machine. By attacking the Soviet Union, Hitler had given Britain a powerful ally. Before the end of 1941 the USA was also at war with Germany. The military advantage was now on the side of the Allies. By 1944 the Soviet Union had been supplied with over 10,000 planes as well as jeeps, lorries, tanks, steel, chemicals, food and clothing. The Soviet Union suffered the brunt of the fighting with Germany during the war; but armed with Allied supplies, they were able to fight on more equal terms.

Hitler had believed that Soviet resistance would crumble within months. Like Napoleon's invasion of Russia over 100 years before, Hitler's invasion proved to be his greatest mistake and eventual undoing.

'Let us defend Mother Volga': a Soviet poster from 1942.

Source E

> The German army in fighting Russia is like an elephant attacking a host of ants. The elephant will kill thousands, perhaps even millions, but in the end their numbers will overcome him, and he will be eaten to the bone.

Colonel von Kleist's warning of the dangers of invading the Soviet Union.

Questions

Section A

1 Why did Hitler decide to invade the Soviet Union?

2 What evidence is there that the Soviet Union was not prepared for the German invasion?

3 Explain the meaning of the terms: **Lebensraum** and **scorched earth**.

Section B

4 Does Source A prove that Hitler was dishonest when he signed the Nazi-Soviet Non-Aggression Pact in 1939? Give reasons for your answer.

5 Until Hitler's invasion of the Soviet Union, Britain's relations with the Soviets had not been good. How does Source C show that relations had changed by 1944?

6 How useful are Sources B, C, D and E in explaining Hitler's failure to defeat the Soviet Union?

7 Source D was produced by the Soviet government as **propaganda** to boost the morale of the Soviet people. Does that mean it is both unreliable and useless to historians?

7.4 New Technology at War

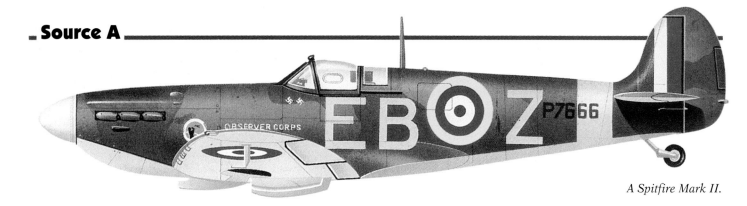

A Spitfire Mark II.

A German armoured vehicle used in the desert war.

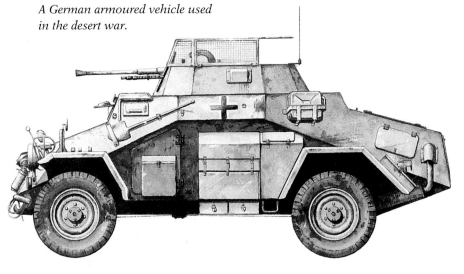

More than any previous war it was a war of machines: tanks and aircraft, motorized columns and heavy artillery, ships and submarines. These weapons of war are products of great scientific inventiveness and technical skill, and depend for their manufacture upon methods of mass production. Countries like Britain, the Soviet Union and the United States possessed both superior resources of manpower and greater industrial potential. Provided these superior resources were properly used, it was inevitable that by the end of 1942 the overall technical advantage in war should swing in favour of the Allies.

From David Thomson, 'Europe since Napoleon', 1966.

A German bomber over London, 1939.

Source E

A Soviet-adapted Sherman tank, 1945.

The Second World War was a very different kind of war from the First. Between 1914 and 1918 the front line hardly changed. Only when Germany was exhausted was the war lost. Both tanks and aircraft were used, but they were not properly developed.

During the twenty years since the end of the First World War, great advances had been made in the **technology of warfare**. Unlike the earlier World War, the Second World War was a war of movement. When Hitler invaded Poland and later France, the Netherlands and Belgium, he used *Blitzkrieg* or 'lightning war' tactics. Motorized columns of armoured cars and tanks sliced through territory, preceded by waves of aircraft. Huge distances were covered within days, and the enemy was quickly defeated.

Once the Allies recovered from early setbacks, they were rapidly able to produce the machines and weapons of war. The Axis powers had to face the resulting onslaught.

The advance in technology had another devastating effect. Like no other previous war it brought home to **civilians** the reality of war. For the people of Great Britain, being surrounded by sea no longer meant that they were safe from attack. Now they could be bombed in their own homes from the air. During the **Blitz** on London thousands were killed in this way. Cities like Coventry and Plymouth were almost destroyed by bombs dropped by German aeroplanes. Even as the Allied armies were closing in on Germany itself in 1944 and 1945, a new and deadly weapon hit London. German scientists had developed the V-1 and V-2 rockets or **flying bombs**. These could be delivered to their targets from launchpads in Europe. As for German civilians they were the victims of even worse bombardment as the aircraft of **Bomber Command** razed cities like **Dresden** to the ground.

Questions

Section A

1 What was *Blitzkrieg*?

2 a How do the sources help to explain why control of the oil supply was so important during the war?

  b How do the sources help to explain why the Allies eventually won the war?

3 Why was it so important for the Allies to have the USA on their side?

Section B

4 What changes took place in warfare between the First World War and the Second World War?

5 Despite the differences between the two world wars, many aspects of war stayed the same. Make a list of some of these aspects.

6 The technological developments in warfare involved great ingenuity and inventiveness. Does this mean that change was for the better? Explain your answer.

7.5 Hiroshima and Nagasaki

On 6 August 1945 a United States B29 bomber plane, the **Enola Gay**, flew over the Japanese city of **Hiroshima**. At 8.15 a.m. an atomic bomb was dropped. It detonated with an explosive power equivalent to 20,000 tons of TNT. Estimates of the casualties vary. The USA gave a figure of 79,400. But the Japanese estimated 240,000 people were either killed in the bombing or died afterwards from the effects of radiation. On 9 August a second bomb was dropped on the port of **Nagasaki**. According to the USA it killed 20,000 people. The Japanese believe 50,000 were killed.

The decision to drop the atomic bomb was taken by the new US President, Harry Truman. he had only been in office for a few months after the death of President Roosevelt. It was a difficult and terrible decision to have to make. Truman received different advice. Those who were against the use of the bomb argued that it was wrong to drop a weapon which would not only destroy buildings but also innocent people. It was expected that the blast alone would do enormous damage and the after-effects of radiation would kill or maim many more, perhaps even future generations. The USA would be accused of a crime against humanity. Those who argued in favour of the bomb pointed out that Japan was already being bombed by conventional weapons and still refused to surrender. Many lives had already been lost winning back control of the Pacific islands, and an invasion of Japan would cost many more lives. It was important to the USA to receive the Japanese surrender. The Soviet Union was preparing to join the war against Japan and it was feared that it might gain control of the country. Furthermore,

Source A

Source B

As we staggered along, we were joined by many who had escaped death for the moment. Many were soldiers who had been out working and had looked up at the blinding flash. They became victims of direct burns. The upper half of their bodies and faces were burned consistently, leaving just the tips of their heads where their caps had protected them. Their skin was charcoal black and hung loosely from their bodies, and body fluid and body oil oozed out.

From June Weden, 'Hiroshima, An Eyewitness Account', 1945.

Source C

The atom bomb was no great decision. It was merely another powerful weapon in the arsenal of righteousness. The dropping of the bombs stopped the war and saved millions of lives.

A comment made later by President Truman.

Source D

It is my opinion that the use of this barbarous weapon was of no material help in our war against Japan. The Japanese were already defeated and were ready to surrender because of the effective sea blockade and the successful use of conventional bombing. The scientists and others wanted to make this test because of the vast sums that had been spent on the project.

Comment by Admiral William D. Leahy, Chief of Staff to the US President in 1945.

The destruction of Hiroshima after the dropping of the atomic bomb on 6 August 1945.

a great deal of money had been spent on developing the weapon and this expense could only be justified if the bomb were dropped.

The Japanese did surrender soon after the atomic bombs were dropped. But historians and others have argued since whether or not this was because of the destruction caused by the bombs.

Source E

A survivor of the bomb at Hiroshima.

Source F

The Japanese were on the verge of surrender. In mid-July they sent out peace feelers via Sato, the Japanese ambassador in Moscow. The Soviets blocked the proposals because they were due to enter the war against Japan three months after VE Day, and they were ready and keen to do so in early August.

General Groves, the engineer director of the US atomic weapons project, was desperate to see the fruits of the project's labours before the end of the war. The military equipment was available and had been developed at a cost of $2000 million. It would have been difficult to justify not using it after such a vast financial investment.

President Truman was very impressed with what he heard. He believed, along with most of his advisers, that if the bomb could be built it should be used. For some reason the scientists failed to mention the long-term dangers of radiation.

From 'Sanity' magazine (Campaign for Nuclear Disarmament), August 1985.

Source G

The Americans would accept nothing less than a full Japanese surrender. The Japanese would not surrender so the Americans planned an invasion of Japan. They knew the Japanese would fight to the last man. An invasion might cost at least two million lives. In the end they decided to use the atom bomb.

From Fiona Reynoldson, 'The War in the East', 1982.

Questions

Section A

1 What do Sources A, B and E tell you about the effects of an atomic explosion?

2 a What differences are there between the US and Japanese accounts of the number of casualties?

 b Suggest reasons why these accounts differ.

3 Compile a list of the arguments used at the time for and against dropping the atomic bomb.

Section B

4 a What are the views expressed in Sources C, D, F and G?

 b Identify and explain which of the above sources are primary and which are secondary.

 c Which secondary source is supported by which primary source?

 d Explain how different views of the past can depend on which primary sources are used.

5 The authors of Source F are campaigners against nuclear weapons today. How is this likely to affect their views on the decision to drop the bombs on Hiroshima and Nagasaki?

7.6 The Holocaust

The 'final solution' of the Jewish question meant the complete extermination of all Jews in Europe. I was ordered to establish extermination facilities at Auschwitz in June 1941. At that time there were already in Poland three other extermination camps: Belzec, Treblinka and Wolzek. I visited Treblinka to find out how they carried out their extermination. The camp commandant told me he had liquidated 80,000 in half a year. He used monoxide gas and I did not think his methods were very efficient. So I used Zyklon B, which we dropped into the death chamber from a small opening. It took from three to fifteen minutes to kill all the people in the death chamber. We knew when the people were dead because their screaming stopped. After the bodies were removed our commandos took off the rings and extracted the gold fillings from the teeth of the corpses. Another improvement we made was to build our gas chambers to take 2000 people at one time.

From the evidence of Rudolf Hess, commandant of Auschwitz, at the Nuremberg Trials of 1945–7.

Source A

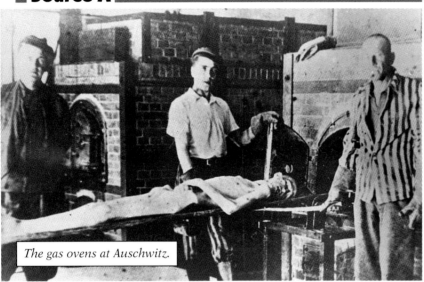

The gas ovens at Auschwitz.

Source C

Dear Kitty, I've got terrible, depressing news today. Our Jewish friends are being taken away by the dozen. They are loaded into cattle trucks and sent to Westerbork, the Jewish camp. It is impossible to escape; most of the people in the camp are branded by their shaven heads. The English radio speaks of Jews being gassed. Elli is very quiet. Her boyfriend has got to go to Germany. Dirk is not the only one: trainloads of boys leave daily.

From 'The Diary of Anne Frank'. Anne was a member of a Dutch Jewish family. She wrote her diary while the family was hiding from the Germans. She was captured and sent to Belsen, where she died of typhus in March 1945, aged 15.

Between 1942 and 1945 the Nazis committed one of the worst acts of barbarism known to humankind. They believed that the Jews were the cause of Germany's problems after the First World War. The idea of the superiority of the Aryan race led to the view that the Jews were inferior. Until 1941 the Jews had been persecuted under the **Nuremberg Laws** which denied them the rights of citizenship. During this time many died in concentration camps through disease and hard labour. It was then that the decision was taken to destroy the entire Jewish race. During the next four years the Nazis were responsible for the deaths of millions of Jews in death camps specially designed to kill as 'efficiently' as possible. Now this is usually referred to as the **Holocaust** a word which stresses the horror experienced by the Jews.

To the Nazis this was the **Final Solution** to the problem of what to do with the Jews. From all over Europe, Jews were rounded up and sent to the death camps in cattle trucks. It is difficult to accept that non-Jewish neighbours did not know the fate of these people. There were some who tried to protect their Jewish friends but many simply turned a blind eye. There is also evidence that the horrific details of the slaughter were known to the British authorities long before they were made public. It was only when the Allied armies liberated Europe in 1945 that the full horror was revealed. It is now estimated that the Nazis were responsible for the deaths of at least six million Jews.

Source D

Since 1942 enormous transports of Jews have come to Auschwitz. A very small number have been sent to the labour camp, while an average of 90 per cent have been taken from the train and killed. The crematorium contains a large hall, a gas chamber and a furnace. People are assembled in a hall which contains 2000 and gives the impression of a swimming bath. They have to undress and are given a piece of soap and a towel as if they are going to the baths. They are then crowded into a gas chamber which is sealed. SS men in gas masks then pour in the poison gas. At the end of three minutes all the bodies are dead. The dead bodies are taken away in carts to the furnace to be burned.

From intelligence reports from Czechoslovakia held by the British Foreign Office, dated 1944.

Source E

The hiring out of concentration camp inmates to industry gives a daily return of six to eight marks of which 70 pfennigs must be deducted for food and clothing. Assuming a camp inmate's life expectation of nine months, the profit is 1431 marks. This can be increased by the rational use of the corpse, i.e. by means of gold fillings, clothing, valuables, etc. On the other hand, every corpse represents a loss of two marks, which is the cost of cremation.

From the notes of an SS officer in the concentration camps.

Questions

Section A

1 What was the Holocaust?

2 Does the Final Solution describe the same events? Explain your answer.

3 Why was the decision taken to order the extermination of the Jews?

4 How likely is it that few people knew at the time what was happening to the Jews?

5 Suggest reasons why few people were prepared to protect the Jews from the Nazis.

Section B

6 What do Sources B and E tell us about the attitudes of those involved in the extermination of the Jews?

7 How useful is Source D to an historian interested in finding out what was known about the Nazi treatment of the Jews by the British authorities?

8 Source C was produced by a 13-year-old Jewish girl in hiding with her family from the Nazis. Does that mean that it can provide no useful and reliable evidence on the Nazi treatment of the Jews?

Source F

Rows of corpses awaiting burial at Belsen death camp, 1945.

7.7 Collaboration and Resistance

What do you think you would do if your country was occupied by foreign forces? You might think that you would be prepared to fight and resist. If you did, you would be risking your life. It might be easier to make the most of your life and keep out of trouble, or even work with the enemy.

These were the difficult choices facing those who lived under **Nazi occupation in Europe**. In most countries there were few who actively resisted, and a few others who worked openly with the occupiers as **collaborators**. Most people, however, just lived their lives as best they could, staying neutral or resisting in a passive and piecemeal way. Even among the resistance forces there were those who only defied the Germans when they were sure that the Allied forces were about to regain control.

Collaborators and traitors

Some people were prepared to work openly with their German rulers. There were those who did business with the Germans and made profits out of the occupation. Some people even helped to round up the Jews for transport to the concentration camps.

Mussert, the leader of the Dutch Fascists, co-operated with the Nazis in the Netherlands and **Pétain** of France set up a police state based in the town of Vichy in co-operation with the Germans. The name of the Norwegian collaborator **Quisling** has passed into the English language as a word meaning 'traitor'.

After the war, known collaborators were attacked, humiliated, put on trial and punished. Quisling and Mussert were executed by their countrymen; Pétain died while serving life imprisonment.

Source A

A 19-year-old French girl who fought with the Resistance.

Source B

A Frenchwoman with a baby is humiliated for befriending Germans, 1945. Notice that her head has been shaved.

Resistance heroes

There were some who were prepared to resist German occupation from the start. Resistance fighters in France and Belgium organized escape routes for Allied airmen. Secret printing presses produced pamphlets to undermine the occupation; factories were sabotaged and railways blown up. By 1944, the **Maquis** (French Resistance) were openly fighting the Germans and sending intelligence reports to the allies in preparation for the **D-Day landings**.

Many of those in the resistance movements hoped to gain power once their country had been liberated. **General de Gaulle** was recognized as the leader of the Free French while in exile in London during the war. He became the President of France after the liberation.

At times different resistance groups fought each other as well as the enemy. In Yugoslavia the Communist resistance fought others who wished to gain control after the defeat of the German occupiers. The leader of the Communists was Marshal Tito who became the long-serving President of Yugoslavia after helping to defeat not only the Germans but also his rivals.

Questions

Section A

1 Explain the meaning of the following terms: **collaboration**; **resistance**.

2 'Most people in German-occupied countries either collaborated with the Germans or resisted them.' Explain whether or not you agree with this statement.

3 Why do you think there were such strong feelings against collaborators after the war?

Section B

4 How might the following have reacted to Nazi occupation of their country?
   a Someone whose father had died fighting the Germans in the First World War.
   b A factory owner supplying boots and shoes.
   c The owner of a cafe.
   d A Communist factory worker.

5 Suggest reasons why some people were actively prepared to resist Nazi occupation and others were not.

Source C

'French Resistance helps throttle the Boche': a French poster by R. Louvat, 1944. Boche was the French name for the Germans.

Source D

The most bitter legacy of German occupation was the civil strife it caused between those who had supported Axis puppet governments or profited from helping the enemy, and those who had engaged in active resistance.

From David Thomson, 'Europe since Napoleon', 1966.

7.8 *Hitler*

Source A

> Until recently Hitler was usually dismissed as a bungling amateur in military matters, utterly out of his depth as a supreme commander, who pulled Germany down to defeat through his irrational conduct of the war. This view of Hitler rests largely on the testimony of certain German generals who rushed into print after the war and blamed the Führer for all that had gone wrong after 1942 while carefully claiming credit for Germany's earlier successes.

From William Carr, 'Hitler: A Study in Personality and Politics', 1978.

This unit on **Adolf Hitler** is the first of a series of four looking at the main war leaders. It is not concerned with the whole of Hitler's life but deals with Hitler as a **military leader**. Few people would question the view that he was a thoroughly evil man who brought death and destruction to millions of people. However, there are differing opinions about his military ability.

Hitler as a military leader

Those who believe that Hitler was a great military leader point to the **success** his forces had in the early part of the war. When he attacked Poland he gambled that France would not come to Poland's aid. His *Blitzkrieg* tactics were devastating in Poland, France, the Netherlands, Belgium and Norway. There were similar successes in Yugoslavia, Greece and North Africa, and in the early part of the war against the Soviet Union. Hitler also performed skilfully in conferences with his generals. He had an excellent grasp of tactics, wide technical knowledge of the German military machine and a powerful memory for detail.

Those who question Hitler's abilities point out his **failures** – especially the failure to defeat Britain and his decision to invade the Soviet Union (see Unit 7.3). They also give the example of his decision to declare war on the USA. Certainly, these errors proved fatal in the end, as the powerful combination of Allies proved too much for the Axis powers. However, it is easy to be wise after the event and point out Hitler's mistakes. It is important to understand that things might have turned out very differently.

Hitler liked to be seen as a strong leader.

Source C

> Almost all those qualified to judge thought that the fighting would be over within a few weeks. No German general expressed doubts, as some had done before the invasion of France. British intelligence gave the Russians ten days.

Comments on Hitler's plans to invade the Soviet Union, from A. J. P. Taylor, 'The Second World War', 1975.

Source D

> If the war is to be lost, the nation will also perish. The nation has proved itself weak. Besides, those who remain after the battle are of little value; for the good have fallen.

Hitler speaking in March 1945.

Source F

Hitler and his generals in conference with the Italian leader, Mussolini, 1941.

Source E

The Führer stresses yet again that the morale of the troops and that of the civilian population affect each other. He is firmly convinced that the troops have infected the civilians with their bad morale, not the civilians the troops. The disaster in the west originated not from the troops, but from the higher-ranking officers.

From 'The Goebbels' Diaries', edited by Hugh Trevor-Roper, 1978. Goebbels stayed loyal to Hitler until the end, although he criticized some of his decisions.

Hitler's thinking

Hitler had weaknesses as a military leader. He had a strong belief that fate had meant him to be great. Encouraged by his early successes he convinced himself that he was a military genius. When things went wrong he blamed others and dismissed them from high command. He was therefore deprived of many able officers. Although he had the ability to inspire others with his confidence, there were few people he could trust and call friends.

Relations between Hitler and his generals were often strained. He was from a humble background and as a soldier had only reached the rank of corporal. His generals were from the upper classes and doubted his military ability. As things started to go wrong on the eastern front, Hitler took more control of decisions himself and became increasingly isolated. He found it difficult to cope with failure. As the Allies closed in on Germany many officers began to think about negotiating peace. They knew that Hitler would not consider it.

One group of officers decided that Hitler had to go. In July 1944, Hitler escaped death from a bomb planted in his headquarters; 160 officers were executed for their part in the plot. When he finally became convinced of defeat he blamed the weaknesses of the German nation and killed himself on 1 May 1945.

Questions

Section A

1 Make a list of Hitler's **successes** and **failures** as a war leader.

2 What were Hitler's **strengths** and **weaknesses** as a military leader?

3 Which of the sources suggest that Hitler was a good war leader? Explain your answer.

Section B

4 What view of Hitler would we get if we only had evidence from Hitler's generals?

5 It is difficult to know who deserves the credit for Germany's early success in the war without more evidence. How might lack of evidence lead to different claims?

6 Show how Sources D and E support the view that Hitler blamed everyone but himself for any failure.

7.9 *Churchill*

To many people living today, **Winston Churchill** was the greatest Prime Minister Britain has ever had. When he died in 1965, two months after his ninetieth birthday, he was given a state funeral usually reserved for royalty. But when war broke out in September 1939, he was not Prime Minister; he was already in his sixties, and thought of by many as a 'has-been'.

Neville Chamberlain tried to prevent the war by appeasing Hitler, while Winston Churchill warned of the dangers of Nazi aggression. Within a few months in 1940 Hitler had invaded Denmark, the Netherlands, Belgium, Norway and France which was on the verge of defeat. Chamberlain had been wrong – he was not the man to lead Britain in wartime. There were calls in Britain for a government of national unity headed by the right man. Churchill was the obvious choice and proved himself to be the ideal war leader. The characteristics he displayed were just what Britain needed. Unlike so many other politicians he warmed to the task of facing the threat from Hitler.

When he became Prime Minister in May 1940, the atmosphere changed overnight. The desks were cleared for action as Churchill took responsibility for the whole conduct of the war. He set the tone for the nation with his inspiring speeches. When the outlook looked bleak, Churchill had every confidence in Britain's ability to resist the Nazi threat and this seemed to infect everyone around him. His inexhaustible stamina and determination were made obvious to all. The image of the cigar and victory sign were ever present in people's imagination. There was no question of defeat.

Source A

Source B

Deeper than the influence of Churchill was the effect of Hitler. His conquest of France and near approach to their shores aroused the British people as no earlier evidence of his tyranny and aggressiveness had done. They reacted once again in their long-bred way, intent to keep their teeth in Hitler's skin at any cost. Never was their collective characterization as a bulldog so clearly demonstrated.

From Basil Liddell Hart, 'History of the Second World War', 1970.

Source C

A British poster featuring and quoting Winston Churchill, 1940.

'All behind you, Winston': a David Low cartoon, 14 May 1940.

Churchill made mistakes. He was impatient. He wanted victory too soon and with inadequate means. The expedition to Greece in April 1941 and the failure to take the Japanese threat to Singapore seriously were certainly mistakes. But he was a man of action; he believed it was better to be doing something and failing than not to do anything at all. His successes outweigh his failures. He kept the morale of the British people high after the 'defeat' of Dunkirk in 1940; he provided the means for the RAF to defeat the Germans during the Battle of Britain in 1940; and he helped to hold the alliance with the USA and the Soviet Union together long enough to defeat Hitler. He sacked many generals but also promoted several successful ones. Perhaps his best appointment was that of **Montgomery**, the hero of El-Alamein. The two shared the same vision of victory.

Source D

Even though large tracts of Europe have fallen into the grip of the Gestapo and Nazi rule, we shall not flag or fail. We shall go on to the end. We shall fight in France, we shall fight in the seas and the oceans, we shall fight with growing confidence and growing strength in the air; we shall defend our island whatever the cost may be. We shall fight on the beaches; we shall fight on the landing grounds, we shall fight in the fields and in the streets, we shall fight in the hills; we shall never surrender.

From a speech by Churchill in 1940.

Source E

Without Churchill, Britain would have fallen in 1940. No other statesman would have created the same faith in victory and inspired the nation to fight on wholeheartedly when all seemed lost. Alone, Winston Churchill saved Western civilization from destruction at the hands of the Nazis.

From Richard Lamb, 'Churchill as War Leader: Right or Wrong?', 1991.

Source F

Churchill, as minister for defence, was no innocent civilian, criticizing strategy from outside, in the way that Lloyd George had been. He was himself an expert on war, or so he believed. He had been a serving army officer; had directed the Admiralty in two world wars; and he now often wore the uniform of an air commodore, the only Prime Minister, not excluding Wellington, to wear military uniform while in office. His mind teemed with original, often with dangerous, ideas, and he could sustain them with technical arguments. The chiefs of staff had difficulty in resisting him.

From A. J. P. Taylor, 'English History 1914–1945', 1965.

Source G

HOLDING THE LINE!

An American poster published in 1942 depicting Churchill as the British Bulldog.

Questions

Section A

1 What qualities did Churchill display as a war leader?

2 Make a list of his successes and failures.

Section B

3 How do you think the British people would have responded to the speech in Source D?

4 According to Source B, what else made the British people determined to resist Hitler?

5 Both Sources B and G refer to the image of the bulldog. One describes the British people and the other Churchill himself. What does this suggest about the relationship between the two?

7.10 Stalin

The Soviet Union bore the brunt of the war against Germany. It has been estimated that 20 million of its soldiers and civilians were killed. The western Soviet Union was in ruins in 1945; 1700 towns and 70,000 villages, six million houses, 32,000 factories, 60,000 kilometres of railway track and 100,000 farms were destroyed or damaged. But after its heavy industry was set up again in the east so that the weapons of war could be built, the country was able to fight back.

Joseph Stalin was the great dictator who led the Soviet Union throughout the 'great patriotic war'. More than any other war leader, he controlled every aspect of running the war. As supreme commander he kept in direct contact by phone with his generals at the front. If things went wrong they were summoned to Moscow to explain their actions to him personally. In the early days of the German invasion those generals whose armies were in retreat were court marshalled and shot. He was ruthless in his determination to defeat the German invaders. At times he gave rash orders with disastrous consequences. At first he made the mistake of believing that his armies needed to be on the offensive. He ordered the attack on Kharkov in March 1942. Refusing to allow any retreat the result was the loss of his armies in the area. In this respect he was partly responsible for the huge loss of life suffered by the Soviet people during the war.

However, he learned to be patient. He soon realized the need to transfer the essential industries to safety beyond the Ural Mountains to the East. He presided over many of the details himself. He also grasped the need for equipment if the Soviet Union was going to strike back at the enemy. The production of tanks and aircraft was made a priority and arrangements were made with the USA to supply essential military equipment. In particular, Stalin wanted trucks. Transporting the troops to the front was vital in such a vast country. This showed his appreciation of the military realities facing the Soviet Union.

As the fortunes of war swung in his favour after the defence of Stalingrad, Stalin gained in maturity as a war leader. He was more prepared to listen to the advice of his generals. At the great tank battle at Kursk in 1943, he allowed the Germans to attack and it was they who tasted defeat. His forces advanced cautiously, pausing whenever there was an obstacle. These were Stalin's direct orders and they worked; one victory followed another as his forces advanced through eastern Europe towards Germany itself.

Source A

It is sometimes asked whether it is possible to slow down the tempo a bit, to put a check on the movement. No, comrades, it is not possible! The tempo must not be reduced. To slacken the pace would mean to lag behind; and those who lag behind are beaten. We do not want to be beaten. Russia was ceaselessly beaten for its backwardness, by Mongol Khans, by Anglo-French capitalists, by Japanese barons. Russia was beaten by all – for its military, cultural, political, industrial, agricultural backwardness. We are 50 or 100 years behind the advanced countries. We must make good this lag in ten years. Either we do it or they crush us.

From a speech by Stalin in 1931.

Source B

An official portrait of Stalin painted in the 1930s.

By 1943 he had become an international statesman. Until 1939, he had never met a minister of another country. Now, he was holding conferences with the British and American leaders on equal terms. He was to show the same determination in conferences as he showed during his war leadership. The desire to beat Hitler was never in doubt. His country suffered much more than those of other leaders. He believed that the Soviet Union must be made safe from any possible attack from the West.

He had warned his people in 1931 of the dangers of being left behind as a weak and backward nation. He was responsible for the deaths of millions as he forced his country to industrialize. There is no question he was a cruel tyrant, but his country emerged from the war as one of the two most powerful countries in the world. Much of the credit for this must go to Stalin himself.

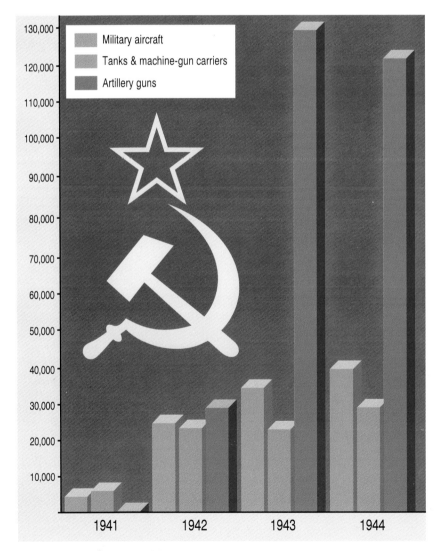

Soviet war production, 1941–44.

Source C

It is fascinating how Stalin piled one position of authority on the other. When the war started, he first of all appointed himself commissar for defence, then he appointed himself commander-in-chief, then he appointed himself supreme commander. Every line of policy ran through Stalin's study. Stalin made every great decision throughout the war and many of the smaller ones too.

From A. J. P. Taylor, 'The War Lords', 1976.

Source D

Stalin was better informed than Roosevelt, more realistic than Churchill – perhaps the most effective of the warlords.

A comment by Averell Harriman, the American Ambassador to Moscow during the Second World War.

Questions

Section A

1 In what ways did the Soviet Union suffer during the war?

2 Why do you think the people of the Soviet Union called the war with Germany the 'great patriotic war'?

3 How do you think Stalin should be remembered? Write an epitaph for him explaining your views of his leadership during the war.

Section B

4 The author of Source D was the American Ambassador to Moscow. Does that mean he can provide reliable evidence of Stalin's ability as a war leader?

5 We do not know who painted Source B. Is it possible then to know whether or not the portrait is reliable?

6 Source C is the only one written by an historian. Is it therefore more reliable and useful as evidence of Stalin than the other sources?

7.11 Roosevelt

President Roosevelt of the USA was unlike the other war leaders in many ways. All the others had done military service while his background had not prepared him for war. The others had a variety of interests while he was a complete politician. He rarely wrote anything, not even his own speeches; the others all wrote books of various kinds.

When the war came he operated in a very individual way. He refused to be hurried into decisions and often acted only at the last moment. He did not like to commit himself to a particular policy. He was always aware of the importance of public opinion. As an elected President he showed great skill in judging the mood of the country. In 1939 he realized the US people wanted little to do with the European war. By 1941 that mood had changed. Public opinion thought that Britain should be helped, although it didn't support US involvement in the war. Roosevelt realized that the war would benefit the USA. The supplies of war materials to aid the Allied war effort also solved unemployment problems and boosted the US economy.

Source A

A British cartoon by Low showing the sadness felt by many that Roosevelt would not be alive to witness the victory he and his country had contributed so much to. April 16, 1945.

Source B

Roosevelt signing the declaration of war against Japan – 1941.

Source C

In the past few years – and most violently in the past few days – we have learned a terrible lesson. We must begin the great task that is before us by abandoning once and for all the illusion that we can ever again isolate ourselves from the rest of humanity. There is no such thing as security for any nation in a world ruled by the principles of gangsterism. There is no such thing as impregnable defence against powerful aggressors who sneak up in the dark and strike without warning. We cannot measure our safety in terms of miles on any map. Modern warfare as conducted in the Nazi manner is a dirty business. We don't like it – we didn't want to get into it – but we are in it, and we are going to fight with everything we've got. We are going to win the war and we are going to win the peace that follows.

From a radio broadcast by Roosevelt in 1941 after the Japanese attack on Pearl Harbor.

After Pearl Harbor his position as President meant he was the commander-in-chief of the armed forces at war. But he spent little time discussing detail with his chiefs of staff and he was not in control of his forces abroad. Often he made decisions without consultation. It was he who decided to send US troops to the Mediterranean in 1943 – he wanted US troops to be fighting before the elections of that year. He hoped this would win him votes. Unlike the other leaders he did not get involved in the details of military tactics. He concerned himself only with the big decisions.

Perhaps the most important of these decisions was to concentrate the war effort against Germany before dealing with Japan. He could see the advantage of extending US influence in Europe. Only the USA would have the resources that Europe would need after the devastation of war. His whole approach to the war was to make sure that the Allies had more of everything than their opponents. He bullied US industry into producing more than anyone thought possible.

He showed great skill in his dealings with people and enjoyed good relationships with his wartime allies. He went out of his way to establish good relations with Stalin. He firmly believed in the idea of the United Nations and had every faith it would work. He was not to live to see the victories against Germany and Japan, nor the souring of relations between the former Allies. By the time he died, suddenly in April 1945, he had led his country out of the Depression of the 1930s to the verge of victory in a major war. The USA was now the single most powerful nation on earth.

Source D

US tanks on the production line during the Second World War.

Source E

Roosevelt proved a superb leader of the American people at war. His buoyant cheerfulness invigorated those who had personal dealings with him, his confident voice brought reassurance and inspiration over the radio. He showed high skill in handling the war effort on a national scale.

From C. P. Hill, 'Franklin Roosevelt', 1966.

Source F

Roosevelt was the greatest American friend we have ever known and the greatest champion of freedom who has ever brought help and comfort from the new world to the old.

Winston Churchill speaking after the death of Roosevelt in April 1945.

Questions

Section A

1 Make a list of the ways in which Roosevelt differed from the other war leaders.

2 Does Source E support Source C in its view of Roosevelt's abilities as a war leader?

3 What do Sources A and F tell us about British attitudes to Roosevelt?

Section B

4 How did each of the following help the Allies to win the war:
- Roosevelt's decisions
- the supply of equipment
- good relations with other leaders?

5 Explain how the factors above are linked.

6 a In what ways do you think the British attitude to Roosevelt might have been similar to the US attitude towards him?
  b In what ways might they have been different?

109

8.1 Evacuation

In the 1930s going to the cinema was very popular. As well as going to see the latest films, people watched newsreels. For the first time they could see the realities of war. They watched in horror as German bombers destroyed the town of Guernica in Spain during the Spanish Civil War.

British people realized that they were no longer safe on their islands. As the war with Germany approached, plans were made to evacuate children and some women from the cities most likely to be targets. In September 1939 these plans were put into effect.

In some cases children would go with their mothers to safer places in the country. Other children were sent away without their parents, who were needed in the cities to work. Sometimes whole schools were moved to safety. Some evacuees were even sent across the Atlantic to Canada. No one was forced to evacuate but there was plenty of encouragement. Many returned home when there were no attacks during the first year of the war. However, when the Germans failed to destroy Britain's air defences in the summer of 1940, Hitler changed tactics. It was decided to switch to bombing raids on cities. From 7 September to 2 November, London was

Source A

There were moving scenes at Gloucester Station yesterday, when 236 mothers and children arrived in the city on the second evacuation train of the day. Several mothers carried babies in their arms, many of whom were crying, and tiny tots held on to their mothers' coats as they were quickly taken to waiting buses. There was, however, a general atmosphere of cheerfulness. Many youngsters seemed to be enjoying the chance of a stay in a new city. It had been arranged to set aside a number of schools for the use of the trainloads of evacuees. Only 236 were on the second train, although the expected number was 800.

From the 'Gloucester Citizen', 3 September 1939.

Source B

Children being evacuated during the 1940–1 Blitz, helped by military policewomen.

bombed every night. This was called the **Blitz**. While many stayed and faced the danger, others were evacuated again.

The experiences of evacuees were many and varied. There are many who have written and talked about their experiences. Many had never seen the countryside before and found it strange and frightening. Separated from their parents and forced to live with strangers, many found it difficult to cope. It was not always easy for the families who received them either. They were expected to provide rooms for the children and to act as foster parents. Some of the children were very poor and were not used to washing and using the toilet. This horrified and upset people in the countryside. Often it could be the other way around. Children from better-off homes in the cities stayed in poor country homes without water and electricity. If the mothers came with the children, they stayed with families, too. With two families in the same house there were often tensions. It was the job of the **billeting officer** to try to help evacuees and their hosts to get on together.

However, many children enjoyed their time away from home. They liked the freedom and the open space of the country. They made friends with the local people. Some enjoyed it so much they would have preferred to stay rather than return home to the city. Some of the evacuees stayed with their adopted families for the whole of the war. There are many examples of lifelong friendships made through evacuation. For many years after the war evacuees would visit their hosts for holidays.

Source C

The German bombing raids continued until well into 1941, when most of the Luftwaffe was needed on the Russian front. London was not the only city to suffer, as the Germans also attacked provincial centres. Hull, Plymouth, Bristol, Liverpool, Manchester and Birmingham were all heavily bombed, but perhaps the most famous of these was Coventry. Coventry was attacked on the night of 14 November 1940 and much of the city was destroyed.

From C. C. Bayne Jardine, 'World War Two', 1968.

Source D

When the school was hit, it was my painful duty to help by picking up any article I saw unearthed as the men dug. I held aloft a small pink purse. No words were needed. The mother of the child to whom it belonged held out her hand, her face so anguished it was frightening to behold. She took it and was led wordlessly away.

Recollections of a London schoolteacher during the Blitz.

Source

A poster of 1941 encouraging evacuation.

Questions

Section A

1 Explain why the cinema pictures of the Spanish Civil War would have helped the government to persuade people to evacuate their children.

2 a Make a list of the good and bad features of evacuation from the point of view of the evacuees.
  b Make a list of the advantages and disadvantages of hosting an evacuee.
  c Explain whether or not you feel evacuation was a good idea.

Section B

3 Does Source B show that children were happy to be evacuated?

4 Do Sources A and E show that not all parents were prepared to evacuate their children?

5 How useful are Sources C and D to an historian studying evacuation? Give reasons for your answer.

6 Source E was produced by the government to encourage evacuation. Does this mean that historians will find it neither useful nor reliable?

8.2 The Role of Women

During the First World War women had played a full part in the war effort. Because of the shortage of men they did many of the jobs usually done by men. Many women worked in the **munitions** factories, making the weapons of war. Male attitudes to women were forced to change. In 1920 women over the age of 30 were entitled to vote in general elections for the first time.

When peace came most women returned to their **traditional roles** of looking after the home and children. Between the wars, many women had paid jobs until they were married. Once they were married they were expected to give up paid work. The jobs women did as clerks, typists, telephonists and nurses were considered suitable only for women. Women's **pay** was much less than men's. For example, a woman teacher earned less than a man doing the same job.

When the Second World War started, women were needed once more to fill the gaps left by men. At first women were encouraged to join the voluntary services: the Auxiliary Territorial Services (ATS), the Women's Royal Naval Service (WRENS) or the Women's Auxiliary Air Force (WAAF). In the ATS many women learned to drive and to service vehicles. Large numbers staffed the anti-aircraft guns. By 1941 the shortage of labour was so serious that women were **conscripted** into the labour force. Unmarried women aged between 20 and 30 now had to work. By July 1943 this was extended to all women not looking after children. They could work either in a weapons factory, in the women's services or on the land.

Most women welcomed the opportunity to work. They particularly enjoyed the opportunity to do 'men's' work. Even those who were not required to work volunteered in their thousands. This often meant that nurseries had to be provided to allow women to work. Women who stayed at home were expected to help out by childminding and taking in laundry.

Women's lives were difficult: after a ten-hour shift in the factory they were still expected to do the shopping and cooking. Women continued to be paid half a man's wage for the same job. They were not allowed to work down the mines (men known as **Bevin Boys** were conscripted for this). When men returned at the end of the war, many women were forced to give up work. But the experience forced a change in attitudes.

A poster of 1943 encouraging women to support the war effort.

A member of the Women's Land Army working on a farm in Watford, 1942.

Source C

Women working in a steel factory in 1943.

Source D

We were given a choice – either the Land Army or munitions. I chose the Land Army. There were about 30 of us girls in a long army hut with a tin roof, divided into rooms with eight beds and a stove in each. It was all very rough and ready, and quite cold in winter. I was a little homesick at first; I'd never been away from home before. Also the work was so strange at first. After a bit I loved it. I was quite upset to come home at the end of the war.

We did what was called 'general farming': milking, snagging turnips, haymaking, harvesting the oats and barley, threshing – that was a dirty job. The girls were from all walks of life, well-to-do, poor, though most were from the local area.

Muriel Taylor from Gateshead, looking back on her days in the Land Army.

Source E

Married women with children were not required to take a job. Women past their early forties were registered but never required to take work. Women over 40 were considered past it! The very idea of registering them aroused great opposition. But it was from these volunteers that the vast majority of munitions workers were recruited. They literally jumped at the idea of going into industry. They were emancipated! Freed from the grinding poverty of the 1930s, released from the kitchen sink, they had a life and money of their own.

A woman clerk in a Welsh employment office commenting in later years on women workers' attitudes during the war.

Source F

The role of women during wartime should not be forgotten, because the output and effort in agriculture and industry greatly contributed to the victory and also began to change male attitudes to women and work. Although we gave up our jobs when the men returned, the experience gave us confidence. The gradual progress of women in industry since 1945 must be connected with this self confidence.

A comment made at a Land Army reunion in 1984.

Questions

Section A

1 According to Source E, why did women want to work?

2 Does Source B help to explain the feelings expressed in Source D? Explain your answer carefully.

3 'The government only encouraged women to work because the war made it necessary.' Using the text and sources, explain whether or not you agree with this view.

Section B

Refer to Unit 3.8 in your answers to the following questions.

4 Draw a timeline to show the changes in women's lives between 1914 and 1945.

5 a How did women's lives change during the Second World War?
   b In what ways did women's lives stay the same?

6 Explain the differences between changes in **experiences** and changes in **attitudes**.

7 Have women enjoyed increasing equality with men since 1914? Explain your answer carefully with examples taken from the text and sources as well as your own knowledge.

8.3 Rationing

Source A

A typical week's supply of rationed food for one adult.

Even before the war the government was afraid of running out of food and other essential goods. Britain relied on much of its food and raw materials coming in from other countries by sea. If the German navy were to sink the ships bringing in supplies, as happened during the First World War, there would be severe shortages. In addition, factories would need to concentrate on war production rather than consumer goods. This would also cause shortages. Because people would not be able to buy whatever they wanted, it was decided that the only fair thing to do was to introduce rationing.

Food rationing

In the early months of the war the German U-boats did even more damage to shipping than had been expected. **Food rationing** was introduced on 8 January 1940. Everyone was given a ration book. People had to register with a grocer and a butcher and receive goods in exchange for the coupons in the ration book and the necessary money. They could only buy food from shops where they were registered.

Fresh foods like fish, bread, fruit and vegetables were not rationed, though some were in short supply. Bananas were hardly ever seen; oranges were reserved for children. The government

Source B

You know that our country is largely dependent on supplies of food from overseas. More than 20 million tons are brought into our ports from all over the world. Our defence plans must therefore provide for the protection of our trade routes by which these supplies come, for reserves of food here and for the fair distribution of supplies both home and imported. During the last eighteen months the government has bought large reserves of essential food. In addition, the necessary arrangements have been made to control the supply and distribution of food throughout the country and to bring in such rationing as may be required.

From a public information leaflet issued by the government in July 1939.

Source C

It was possible to buy most things from people who got them on the black market. My mother would have nothing to do with it. I remember that once my father arrived with a bottle of milk which had been offered in a pub. He had paid eightpence for it, a very high price at the time. My mother was so cross with him that he felt ashamed and never did it again.

From D. J. Steel and L. Taylor, 'The Steels', 1976.

Source D

Out from the kitchen came my mother with tea, dinner and supper, all in one, on two tin trays. This was her finest hour, her triumph over adversity and the Germans. Like animals we set about devouring the meal. First there was corned beef stew lapping dumpling islands made of soyabean flour. Or whalemeat steaks which they said did not taste of fish.

Many families ate horsemeat but my mother refused to buy it. To her every horse was Black Beauty and the thought of eating horse was as repugnant as eating dog. With the stew was a vegetable, curly kale perhaps, or home-grown spinach. Nettles were also tried as a vegetable.

From Derek Lambert, 'The Sheltered Days', 1991.

launched a campaign to encourage people to '**Dig for Victory**' and grow their own vegetables. This was very successful, and the government urged people to eat as many vegetables as possible.

Many shopkeepers kept unrationed food **under the counter** and only sold it to regular customers.

In November 1941 an additional type of food rationing was introduced. As well as the weekly ration, people were given a number of points per month. They could use these to buy foods such as biscuits and cereals if they were available.

It usually fell to women to do the shopping and cooking, and many used great ingenuity with few resources. Magazines were full of ideas and advice to make food go further and still be interesting. In fact, it has been suggested that during the war people were far **healthier** than before or since. Not only did rationing make sure that food was given out fairly, but people were also eating a more balanced diet.

Rationing of other goods

Before long there were few new items on the shop shelves. Rationing of clothes was introduced as early as June 1940. Fuel was needed in factories, so **coal** for home use was rationed in July 1941. Water, too, was in great demand to cool the machines producing weapons. It was difficult to get the materials to make soap. **Water** and **soap** were therefore added to the list. No one was allowed more than 13 cm of water in their weekly bath.

To win the war everything had to take second place to war production. People were prepared to make sacrifices as long as goods in short supply were distributed fairly. However, it was possible to buy most things if you had the money and knew who to ask. There was a **black market** in stolen and shortage goods. Those who operated it risked severe penalties in selling goods for more than the government's fixed price. Generally only the wealthy could afford to buy in this way.

Source E

Everyone was allowed 60 clothes coupons for the year in 1940 (later reduced to 48).

A woman's coat	14 coupons
A man's coat	16 coupons
A dress	11 coupons
A pair of shoes	5 coupons

Examples of clothes rationing.

Questions

Section A

1 Explain the meaning of the following terms: **rationing**; **under the counter**; **black market**.

2 Using the text and sources, draw up a weekly wartime menu for a single adult. Use only the types and amounts of food you know were available.

3 How might you have used your 60 clothes coupons in 1940?

4 Why do you think the woman in Source C was so angry with her husband?

Section B

5 Why did the government introduce rationing?

6 Were fuel and clothes rationed for the same reasons as food? Explain your answer.

7 One of the consequences of food rationing was that people were healthier. Suggest other consequences.

8.4 Civil Defence

When the war broke out the government put into effect a number of plans to defend the country. It tried to find the best ways to protect people from possible air attack and invasion. This is known as **civil defence**. All governments have such plans, even in peacetime.

We have seen that many children and their mothers were evacuated. But this was just one aspect of civil defence.

Air-raid precautions

In case of air attack, an **early warning system** had to be understood by all. The government published leaflets explaining how it worked. Everybody, including babies, had a gas mask. The government provided materials for shelters to be put up in people's gardens. These were known as **Anderson shelters**, after the government minister responsible for them. The newly developed **radar system** gave early warning of enemy aircraft. Sirens were sounded, and people made for the shelter until the 'All Clear' signal.

An important job was done by **Air-Raid Protection** (ARP) wardens. They were local people who attended the scene of an explosion and called the ambulance, fire and rescue services. It could be a dangerous job. Air-raid wardens were expected to investigate unexploded bombs and call the bomb disposal squad if necessary.

Wardens also had to enforce the **blackout regulations**. Most German air attacks were at night. It was vital that no light should be seen which the enemy planes might use to target certain areas. It became an offence to have a light showing after dark. This made life very difficult, and there were many accidents in the dark.

'Dad's Army'

Most civil defence was concerned with air attack, but other actions were taken in case of invasion. The government organized people to dig trenches, erect pillboxes and remove road signs. **Local Defence Volunteers** spent their spare time on duty. These were men who were, for example, too old to be called up to fight. To begin with, they were jokingly known as 'Dad's Army'. They were given no weapons or uniforms and could be seen marching with any substitute for a weapon. Churchill suggested that **Home Guard** was a better name, and their image gradually changed. Gradually they were properly organized and equipped like the full-time army to defend Britain against the invasion which never came.

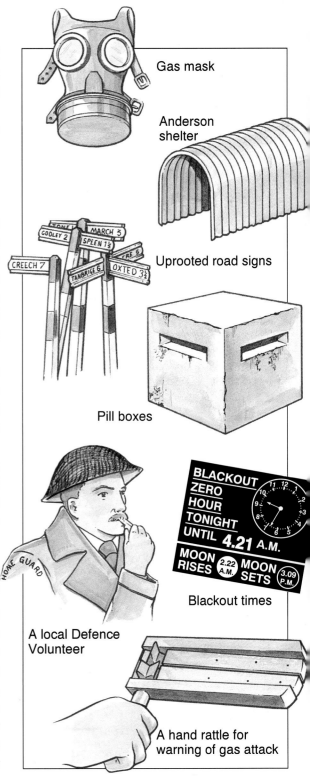

Gas mask

Anderson shelter

Uprooted road signs

Pill boxes

BLACKOUT ZERO HOUR TONIGHT UNTIL **4.21** A.M.
MOON RISES 2.22 A.M. MOON SETS 3.09 P.M.

Blackout times

A local Defence Volunteer

A hand rattle for warning of gas attack

Features of the government's wartime civil defence programme.

Source A

AIR-RAID WARNINGS

When air raids are threatened, warning will be given in towns by sirens or hooters, which will be sounded, in some places by short blasts, and in other places by a warbling note, changing every few seconds. In war, sirens and hooters will not be used for any other purpose than this. The warning may also be given by the police or air-raid wardens blowing short blasts on whistles. When you hear the warning, take cover at once.

Remember that most of the injuries in an air raid are caused not by direct hits by bombs, but by flying fragments of debris or bits of shells. Stay under cover until you hear the sirens or hooters sounding continuously for two minutes on the same note, which is the signal 'Raiders Passed'. If poison gas has been used, you will be warned by means of hand rattles. Keep off the streets until the poison gas has been cleared away. Hand bells will be rung when there is no longer any danger. If you hear the rattle when you are out, put on your gas mask at once and get indoors as soon as you can.

LIGHTING RESTRICTIONS

All windows, skylights, glazed doors or other openings which would show a light will have to be screened with dark blinds or blankets, or brown paper pasted on the glass, so that no light is visible from outside. You should obtain now any materials you may need for this purpose. No outside lights will be allowed, and all street lighting will be put out. Instructions will be issued about the dimming of lights on vehicles.

From a public information leaflet issued by the government in July 1939, shortly before the outbreak of war.

Questions

Section A

1 Explain how the early warning system was designed to save lives.

2 Why were road signs removed?

3 The Germans never used gas in any attack on Britain. Does this mean that the issue of gas masks was a waste of time and money? Explain your answer.

Section B

4 Using the text and the sources, list the precautions taken by the government and the people in case of:
  a air attack;
  b invasion.

5 a Which of the items in the drawing on page 116 could be used in case of both air attack and invasion?
  b Explain how they were used.

6 Suggest reasons why some people might have been prepared to join the ARP or the Home Guard and others were not.

Source B

An ARP warden on duty in London, in 1940.

Source C

The section had no arms or ammunition. The most useful early weapons were pickaxe handles with the heads drilled and filled with a couple of pounds of molten lead. Even after rifles were issued some older members preferred to carry loaded pickaxe handles rather than firearms during night patrol.

A member of the Home Guard remembers the early days of the war.

9.1 Yalta and Potsdam

Yalta

By February 1945, Germany was in retreat on all fronts. As their troops closed in, the Allied leaders met at **Yalta** in the Crimea. The **'Big Three'** – Roosevelt for the USA, Churchill for Britain and Stalin for the Soviet Union – met to discuss the future of Europe after Hitler was defeated.

The leaders came to a number of agreements. Germany was to be disarmed and divided into four zones of occupation, governed by Britain, the USA, France and the Soviet Union. Nazism was to be stamped out, and the Nazi leaders put on trial. Germany would be forced to pay reparations, of which half would go to the Soviet Union. Poland was to give back land taken from Russia in 1921. In return, Poland was to receive land taken from Germany. Finally, countries occupied by Germany were to be free to elect their own governments. These agreements hid the fact that the Western leaders were deeply suspicious of each other.

The Soviet Union had lost 20 million lives during the war. Stalin was determined to keep control of those areas occupied by the Red Army. He hoped that this would keep his country safe from attack from the West. The Western leaders feared the spread of **communism** and wanted free elections in Soviet-occupied territory. By the time the Allies met again it was clear that the alliance which had defeated Hitler had been replaced by distrust and suspicion. The hostile relations between West and East after the war became known as the **cold war**.

Potsdam

The venue for the next meeting, held in July 1945, was **Potsdam**, on the outskirts of Berlin. By this time many changes had taken place. Roosevelt had died in April, and was replaced by **Harry Truman**. Churchill had been defeated in a general

Source A

The Germans invaded the USSR through countries whose governments were hostile to the Soviet Union. And so what can be surprising about the fact that the Soviet Union, anxious for its future safety, is trying to see that governments loyal to the Soviet Union should now exist in those countries.

A speech by Stalin explaining the Soviet attitude to the forms of government proposed for Eastern Europe.

Source B

At the present moment in world history nearly every world nation must choose between alternative ways of life. One way is based on the will of the majority, and has free elections, representative government, freedom of speech and religion.

The second is based on the will of a minority imposed by force on the majority. It relies on terror and oppression, control of the press and radio, fixed elections, and the suppression of freedom.

It will be the policy of the US to support free peoples.

President Truman sets out his policy to oppose communism in Eastern Europe, 1948.

Source C

Churchill, Roosevelt and Stalin at the Yalta conference in February 1945.

The division of Germany at the end of the Second World War.

Source D

From Stettin in the Baltic to Trieste in the Adriatic, an iron curtain has descended. Behind that line, all the capitals of the states of central and eastern Europe are subject in one form or another not only to Soviet influence but to a high and increasing measure of control from Moscow.

Winston Churchill, speaking at Fulton, Missouri, in 1946.

Questions

Section A

1 Explain the meaning of the following terms: **cold war**; **iron curtain**; **Berlin Wall**.

2 What decisions were made about the future of Germany at the Yalta conference?

3 Make a list of the important events between the meetings at Yalta and Potsdam.

4 How did Germany become two separate nations after the war?

Section B

5 Why was Stalin determined to keep control of those countries occupied by the Red Army at the end of the war?

6 Why did the Western leaders want free elections in eastern Europe at the end of the war?

7 Study the following factors:
● the Soviet Union and the USA had different traditions and systems of government
● the defeat of Germany removed the reason for the alliance between the Soviet Union and the West.
Which of the factors is a short-term reason for the cold war and which is a long-term reason? Explain your answer.

8 Was any one country to blame for the cold war? Explain your answer.

election, and Britain was now represented by the Labour leader, **Clement Attlee**. Germany had surrendered in May 1945, and the Red Army now occupied territory deep inside Germany. On the day the conference opened, the USA carried out the first ever test explosion of the atomic bomb.

Truman thought he could insist on free elections in Poland and other eastern European countries. Stalin had made his position clear by arresting non-Communist Polish leaders and setting up a Communist government in Poland. The meeting broke up without agreement on this issue. Instead, the arrangements concerning Germany agreed at Yalta were confirmed.

Europe divided

In fact, the future of Europe had been decided by the positions of the Allied armies at the end of the war. It was soon clear that Stalin would insist on controlling the areas of eastern Europe recaptured by the Red Army. There was nothing the USA could do, short of declaring war on the Soviet Union. Europe was split in two, and Churchill's '**iron curtain**' now separated two very different political systems (see Source D).

Nowhere was this more obvious than in Germany. The Allied commanders could not agree on the running of Germany as a single nation, and it became two separate countries. The Soviet zone became East Germany; the British, French and US zones became West Germany. In 1961 the Communists built the **Berlin Wall** across the city to stop people escaping to the West from the Soviet East. The division of East and West was now set in concrete.

9.2 The Marshall Plan

Europe in ruins

It is difficult to imagine the cost of the Second World War. It has been estimated that in the 2000 days of war, 500 European lives were lost every hour. Perhaps as many as 50 million people died in all. In addition Europe lay in ruins. Factories, cathedrals, roads, railways and harbour installations were smashed beyond repair. In the countryside, vast areas of farmland had been the battlegrounds of opposing armies. Food production had been severely affected; in 1945 Europe was producing only 30 per cent of the wheat grown in 1938. Millions of people had lost their homes and possessions. As many as a quarter of all the houses in Germany had been destroyed. Great cities in France, Belgium, the Netherlands and Italy were reduced to rubble. Warsaw, Budapest, Belgrade and Leningrad had received terrible poundings.

There were also almost 8 million **refugees** or 'displaced persons' in Europe at the end of the war. They were survivors from the death camps and German-speaking people driven out of eastern Europe by the Soviet Army. Many returned home after a few months or were resettled in North America, Australia or western Europe. As many as 300,000 spent years in refugee camps in Germany and Austria.

Who would pay?

At first millions of dollars worth of reparations were demanded from Germany. It was agreed that the Soviet Union would receive the greatest compensation. This did not last long. As suspicion of the Soviets grew, there were calls for a new policy. Britain, France and the USA decided that Germany's economy had to be re-established to provide a buffer between the West and the Soviet-dominated East. Also, people feared that other European countries would be taken over by Communists as long as their economies were in ruins. The question to be answered was, who was going to pay?

Britain was in no position to provide aid. Britain's own economy had been brought close to bankruptcy,

Source A

The world situation is very serious: the loss of life, the destruction of cities, factories, mines and railroads, the dislocation of the entire fabric of the European economy. So Europe must have substantial help or face very serious economic, social or political problems.

The United States should do whatever it is able to do to help the return of normal economic health in the world. Our policy is directed not against any country or doctrine but against hunger, desperation and chaos.

US Secretary of State George C. Marshall puts forward his plan in 1947.

Source B

Do not sow seed. I will sell you maize.

Do not build new shipyards. I will sell you old ones cheaply.

Why do you want to strengthen your currency? Why don't you try mine?

It is difficult to carry out your policy? Carry out ours!

A Soviet view of the Marshall Plan, 1948.

Source C

Refugees forced to migrate to the West in 1945.

and rationing had to continue after the war. The only country with the resources was the USA. The war had saved the USA from the Depression of the 1930s. There was no fighting on American soil, and the USA had supplied the Allies with the weapons to win the war. It had become a **superpower**, with the world's most powerful economy and military capacity.

Involvement in the war had shaken the USA out of isolation. Now the fear of communism and the wish to find markets for US goods were enough to persuade the USA to take on the role of resisting the spread of communism worldwide.

The **Marshall Plan** was announced in June 1947. Billions of dollars would be made available to those countries prepared to co-operate with each other to bring about general economic recovery in Europe. In return, countries would be expected to buy US goods and provide opportunities for US investment.

Even the Soviet Union asked about the terms of Marshall Plan membership. When they found the terms unacceptable, the Soviets would not take part and refused to allow other countries in eastern Europe to attend discussions. Instead only western European countries agreed to the terms. All that remained was for the US Congress to agree to provide the money. When Czechoslovakia fell under Communist control in February 1948, Congress was persuaded to provide £4 billion for the first year.

Source D

The Marshall Plan will mean placing European countries under the economic and political control of the USA.

This plan is also an attempt to split Europe into two camps and, with the help of the United Kingdom and France, to complete the formation of a bloc of several European countries hostile to the interests of the democratic countries.

From a speech at the United Nations by the Soviet Deputy Foreign Minister in 1947.

Questions

Section A

1 Why were there so many refugees in Europe at the end of the war?

2 How does the Soviet view of the Marshall Plan given in Sources B and D differ from the US view expressed in Source A?

Section B

3 Study the following list of factors:
- The economies of Europe were in ruins.
- Britain was almost bankrupt.
- The USA feared Communist take-overs in Europe.
- The USA wanted European markets for its goods.
- Europe had to be strong to resist the Soviet Union.
- The USA had emerged from the war as the world's greatest power.
- The USA was prepared to take the responsibility for the recovery of Europe.

  a Make two lists of the factors under the headings **political** and **economic**.
  b Are any of the factors linked as causes of the Marshall Plan?
  c Are the political causes of the Marshall Plan more important than the economic ones? Explain your answer.

9.3
Superpower Rivalry and the New Europe

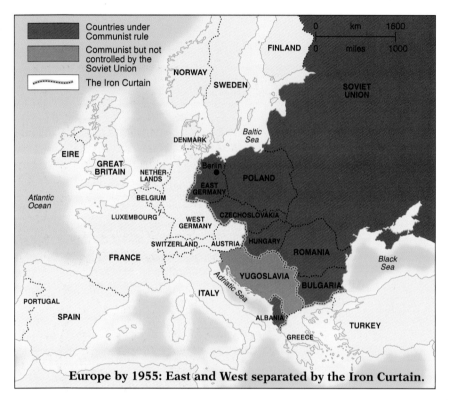

Europe by 1955: East and West separated by the Iron Curtain.

Map key:
- Countries under Communist rule
- Communist but not controlled by the Soviet Union
- The Iron Curtain

0 km 1600
0 miles 1000

FINLAND
NORWAY
SWEDEN
SOVIET UNION
DENMARK
Baltic Sea
EIRE
GREAT BRITAIN
NETHER-LANDS
Berlin
POLAND
EAST GERMANY
Atlantic Ocean
BELGIUM
LUXEMBOURG
WEST GERMANY
CZECHOSLOVAKIA
SWITZERLAND
AUSTRIA
HUNGARY
FRANCE
ROMANIA
Black Sea
YUGOSLAVIA
BULGARIA
ITALY
Adriatic Sea
PORTUGAL
SPAIN
ALBANIA
TURKEY
GREECE

Source A

The Second World War dislodged Western Europe from its position at the centre of world politics. Its great powers no longer had any influence in the east of the continent. Its overseas empires were beginning to crack up as nationalists in the colonies took advantage of their weakened masters. Some of its more far-sighted politicians believed that the best hope for the future lay in some form of economic and political union of the separate states.

From Tony Howarth, 'The World since 1900', 1979.

Source B

Events in Czechoslovakia in 1948 and the Berlin blockade caused a more definite attitude in the United States. The result was the formation of the North Atlantic Treaty Organization in April 1949. It included not only members of the Brussels Pact and the United States, but also Canada, Denmark, Norway, Iceland, Italy and Portugal.

From H. L. Peacock, 'Europe and Beyond', 1974.

There were no superpowers in 1914. Instead, there were a number of great powers of similar strength. These included Britain, France, Germany, Italy, Russia, Austria-Hungary, the USA and Japan. By 1945 this had changed. Austria-Hungary had been broken up after the First World War. Germany, Italy and Japan had been crushed in the Second World War. France was weakened by four years of Nazi occupation, and Britain emerged from the war exhausted and almost bankrupt. On the other hand, both the Soviet Union and the USA were so much stronger in 1945 than the other nations that they were called **superpowers**.

We have seen how the friendship between the two superpowers did not last after 1945 (see Unit 9.1). The many differences in the ways these two countries were run prevented there being much understanding of each other. It was soon clear that the war was being replaced by a very **uneasy peace**.

Source C

The USA had once preferred to keep out of world affairs. Now it was prepared to use its great power to resist Soviet influence all over the world. The Soviet Union was determined to keep control over those countries in Eastern Europe which it had overrun in 1945.

The new superpowers became locked in a power struggle. This was all the more dangerous with the development of **atomic weapons**. In 1945 the USA was the only country which possessed these weapons, but in 1949 the Soviet Union exploded its first atomic bomb.

The Berlin blockade and NATO

The tension between the two countries had already shown itself in a dangerous form. In 1948 the Soviets had tried to take the whole of **Berlin** under their control. Even though Berlin was deep inside the Soviet zone of Germany, it had been agreed that control of the city would be shared between Britain, France, the Soviet Union and the USA. In June 1948 the Soviet Union cut Berlin off from West Germany. Determined to keep their influence in Berlin, the Western powers organized an **airlift** to supply their sectors. In May 1949 an agreement was reached to reopen the land routes to the city. The Soviets had been forced to accept the continued existence of a separate West Berlin.

To counter what they saw as the Soviet threat, many Western countries formed the **North Atlantic Treaty Organization (NATO)** in April 1949. This was a military alliance. The Soviet Union responded with its own defensive alliance of Eastern European states: the **Warsaw Pact**, formed in 1955.

The division of Europe between East and West was really between those countries that looked to the USA for protection and those countries under the influence of the Soviet Union. The countries of western Europe could no longer afford to have rivalries among themselves. They had to learn to co-operate in a wider community.

Source D

The parties agree that an armed attack against one or more of them in Europe or North America shall be considered an attack against them all.

The most important clause of the NATO treaty, 1949.

A cartoon drawn by a child during the Berlin blockade. It gives thanks to the pilots for the airlift of supplies.

Questions

Section A

1 Study the map carefully.
   a What was the line separating eastern Europe from the West called?
   b Which countries were under Soviet control by 1955?
   c Which communist country stayed free of Soviet control?

2 What do the initials NATO stand for?

3 What was the Berlin airlift and why was it important?

Section B

4 In what ways had the power held by different countries in 1914 changed by 1945?

5 In 1914 the world's great powers were often suspicious of each other, and groups of nations formed alliances against others. How had this changed by the 1950s and in what ways had it remained the same?

6 How had the USA's attitude to its role in Europe changed after the Second World War?

7 Explain how the Second World War changed relations between:
   a the USSR and western Europe, and
   b the western European countries themselves.

8 Was the Europe of 1950 a safer or a more dangerous place to live in than the Europe of 1900? Explain your answer, using the text and sources for support.

9.4 The United Nations

'The Trustees of Humanity', a cartoon by Zec, 1945.

As early as 1943 the USA, the Soviet Union, Britain and China had decided that a new international body should replace the **League of Nations**, which had failed to stop the war. In June 1945, 50 nations signed the **United Nations Charter**. The **UN General Assembly** met for the first time in London in January 1946 and decided that its permanent home should be in New York.

The main purpose of the UN was to prevent conflict and to keep peace between nations. The League of Nations had tried to do the same but failed to prevent powerful nations attacking defenceless ones. The UN was given greater powers to agree to the use of force if necessary.

Hopes and disappointment

Britain, France, the Soviet Union and the USA had permanent positions on the UN **Security Council**. People hoped they would work together for world peace. But relations between the Soviet Union and the West grew worse at the end of the war. The UN could only work if Security Council members agreed. Any member of the Security Council could use its **veto** (the right to say 'no') to block a recommended action.

Another problem was that a permanent seat on the Security Council had been given to **Nationalist China** in 1945. In 1949 the Nationalists had fled into exile on the island of Formosa (Taiwan), after the **Communist** take-over of mainland China; yet the Nationalists kept the Security Council seat until 1971.

For these reasons the UN has often been bypassed and ignored by many nations: many conflicts have taken place despite its efforts. The two superpowers soon preferred to deal directly with each other rather than through the UN.

On the other hand, the UN has achieved a great deal. It has many agencies like the **International Labour Organization** and the **World Health Organization** which do tremendous work to tackle human problems in an international way. It encourages its members to understand each other through meeting and talking – allowing them the opportunity to talk rather than fight. When it has failed, this has been because countries put their own interests first.

The General Assembly of the United Nations approved by a large majority the issue of the Declaration of Human Rights, the first international Bill of Rights in history. It consists of a preamble and 31 articles which lay down certain general principles, including the condemnation of slavery and torture, the universal recognition of the right to a fair trial and the freedom of expression, of religion, of association and of peaceful assembly. The rights are not guaranteed by legal sanctions, but each nation signing the Declaration was required to agree to bring its own laws into line with all its clauses.

From John Wroughton and Denys Cook (eds.), 'Documents on World History', 1976.

The various bodies of the UN and their duties.

Source C

A UN soldier on duty in the Lebanon, 1991.

Questions

Section A

1 Study the diagram of the organization of the UN carefully.
  a Briefly explain the duties of the different branches of the UN.
  b How are the branches of the UN linked with each other? Use examples of connections between each branch to explain your answer.
  c Which of the branches of the UN do you think is the most powerful? Give reasons for your answer.

2 What is the main purpose of the UN?

Section B

3 Draw a diagram to show the different types of work done by the UN.

4 Explain the links between the different jobs carried out by the UN.

5 Suggest reasons why some people thought the UN a success while others considered it a failure.

9.5 *The Welfare State*

An unemployed miner in Wigan in 1939.

In the 19th century, governments felt that they had few responsibilities for their citizens. People were expected to provide for themselves. Slowly, however, these *laissez-faire* attitudes changed. During the 20th century the government took on more and more responsibilities.

By 1939 Britain already had a National Insurance scheme providing cover for some workers in case of unemployment and sickness. Old-age pensions and compulsory education up to the age of 14 had also been introduced.

The war gave people the feeling of **working together** against a common enemy. It brought people from different social classes into close contact. Many people from better-off backgrounds came face to face with poverty for the first time. This was especially true of those who were involved with evacuation. They realized how many people were still deprived of basic needs. Also, to run the war effectively the government took on **emergency powers**. Soon the government was using this extra influence to provide free help to those most affected by the war.

The Beveridge Report

In 1942 **Sir William Beveridge** published his report on **social security**. In it he identified the **five 'giants' of poverty** which he believed were unacceptable in a country like Britain: these were want, disease, squalor, ignorance and idleness.

Beveridge suggested ways to defeat these problems: a new health service for all citizens; more and better housing; more and better schools; full employment; and a wider National Insurance scheme to provide basic needs when individuals were unable to earn enough to look after themselves and their families.

Source C

A 'Punch' cartoon of 1949 criticizing the welfare state.

Source A

> The day is here! For years the reformers of all parties have tried to safeguard the aged, the poor and the sick. Much has been done – much more than in any other large country. But always you wanted fuller protection against misfortune. You wanted the state to accept larger responsibility for the individual citizen who served it faithfully. You wanted social security. From this day onwards, you have it.

From the 'Daily Mirror', 5 July 1948, the official start to the welfare state in Britain.

What Beveridge was proposing was a **welfare state**, whereby the government would take responsibility for every citizen 'from the cradle to the grave'. This did not mean that people would get something for nothing. Instead, contributions would be taken from every wage and salary to pay for services. Other services would be paid for by taxes and local rates. It would be the government's job to collect the money and spend it to provide the services.

These ideas were not entirely new. But when the war came to an end, it was clear that people expected a better life from the victory over Hitler. Soldiers returning from the front felt this especially strongly. People thought the **Labour Party** would do most to bring about the welfare state they wanted. In the general election of July 1945 Labour won a massive victory.

The Conservatives had already begun to put some of Beveridge's proposals into practice with the Education Act of 1944. The Prime Minister, Winston Churchill, was also planning a programme of house building. But it was left to the new Labour government to try to complete the work.

Labour set up the new **National Insurance** scheme to provide a range of benefits for those who might suffer loss of earnings for any number of reasons; and there was a new plan to produce good-quality **council housing**. In 1948 Labour set up the **National Health Service**. Some people criticized the welfare state, because they believed people would be too dependent on the state and not help themselves. However, the majority of people supported it.

▬ Questions ▬

Section A

1 Match the five 'giants' of poverty with the proposals to solve them described in this unit.

2 Use the text and sources to explain what is meant by the **welfare state**.

3 What effect did the war have on people's wish to have a welfare state?

4 How were health services to be paid for after 1948?

Section B

5 Sources B and D are photographs. Does that mean they provide reliable evidence of the need for the welfare state?

6 Source A is taken from a newspaper which supported the introduction of the welfare state. Does this mean it can provide no useful and reliable evidence?

7 Source C is a cartoon. Does that mean that historians trying to find evidence of attitudes to the welfare state would not find this source useful?

8 'Photographs are more reliable sources of evidence than other types of sources.' Explain whether or not you agree with this statement.

▬ Source D ▬

A poor family living in a single room in a slum in Newcastle in the 1930s.

Heinemann Educational
a division of Heinemann Publishers (Oxford) Ltd,
Halley Court, Jordan Hill, Oxford OX2 8EJ

OXFORD LONDON EDINBURGH
MADRID ATHENS BOLOGNA PARIS
MELBOURNE SYDNEY AUCKLAND SINGAPORE
TOKYO IBADAN NAIROBI HARARE
GABORONE PORTSMOUTH NH (USA)

First published 1993
93 94 95 11 10 9 8 7 6 5 4 3 2 1

British Library Cataloguing in Publication Data is available from
the British Library on request.

ISBN 0 435 31212X

Designed and produced by Visual Image, Street, Somerset

Originated by Monarch Litho Gravure Ltd, Bristol

Printed and bound in Hong Kong
Produced by Mandarin Offset

Acknowledgements

The authors and publisher would like to thank the following for
permission to reproduce photographs:
Associated Press/Topham: 9.4C
Archiv Für Kunst and Geschichte: 5.1A, 5.4C
Arxiu Mas/The Prado, Madrid © DACS 1993: 6.3D
Bibliothèque Nationale: 7.7C
Bildarchiv Preussischer Kulturbesitz: 5.5C
Bridgeman Art Library: 2.2A
British Library: 1.1A, 1.3D, 1.3F, 2.7B, 2.8C
Bundesarchiv, Koblenz: 5.5A
Camera Press: 7.4D, 7.6F
Jean-Loup Charmet: 3.9E
Communist Party Library: 5.1B
Conservative Party Archives: 5.3A
Daily Mirror: 9.4A
Edimedia: 1.2D
Heeresgeschichtliches Museum: 1.2A, 2.4B, 2.6C
Hulton Picture Company: 3.5A, 5.2A, 5.7D, 7.8F, 8.1B, 9.5B
Hulton Picture Company/Bettman Archive: 4.3C
Robert Hunt Library: 8.2C
Imperial War Museum: Title page, 2.2B, 2.2K, 2.8A, 2.9B, 3.1B, 3.2B, 3.2C, 3.3A, 3.3E,
    3.4A, 3.4D, 3.5B, 3.6C, 3.6D, 3.6E, 3.7A, 3.8C, 3.8D, 3.10D, 3.10E, 7.2A, 7.2C, 7.6F,
    7.7A, 7.9C, 7.11D, 8.1E, 9.1C
Keystone: 7.8B
David King Collection: 7.3D

Magnum Photos Ltd: 7.5E, 7.7B, 8.4B
Mansell Collection: 5.6D
Mary Evans Picture Library: 2.5A, 2.5B, 3.1D, 3.1H, 3.9C
Military Archive and Research Services: 5.4A
Moro, Roma: 5.2B
Museo del Risorgimento, Milan: 7.3C, 8.2A
National Army Museum: 2.4H
Novosti Press Agency: 5.6A
Peace Pledge Union: 3.7B, 3.7D
Peter Newark's Military Archive: 3.6F, 7.2C, 7.9G, 7.10B, 7.11B
Punch: 2.8D, 6.2A, 6.3A, 6.5F, 9.5C
Robert Opie Collection: 3.1A, 3.1E, 5.7B, 5.7C, 8.3A
Suddeutscher Verlag: 9.2C
David Taylor: 4.1A, 4.1C, 4.1F
Topham Picture Library: 6.5B
Ullstein Bilderdienst: 7.6A
University of Kent: 4.2A, 6.2B, 6.2E, 7.9A, 7.11A
Victoria and Albert Museum: 6.1A

Cover photo: German soldier looking over a ruined village in
France. This photograph is taken from *Signal*, Hitler's wartime
propaganda magazine.

Every effort has been made to contact copyright holders of
material reproduced in this book. Any omissions will be rectified
in subsequent printings if notice is given to the publisher.

Details of Written Sources

Barry Bates, *The First World War*, Blackwell, 1984: 2.4F; C. C. Bayne Jardine,
Mussolini and Italy, Longman, 1966: 5.2E; C. C. Bayne Jardine, *World War Two*,
Longman, 1968: 7.3B, 7.3E, 8.1C; Sidney Bradshaw Fay, *Origins of the World War*,
Collier Macmillan, 1966: 1.3H; Josh Brooman, *Hitler's Germany*, Longman, 1985: 7.6B;
William Carr, Hitler: *A Study in Personality and Politics*, Arnold, 1978: 7.8A; S. Case,
The First World War, Evans, 1976: 2.2G; Christopher Culpin, *Making History*,
Collins Educational, 1984: 4.3A, 6.4B; *Daily Mirror*, 15 January 1918: 3.4B;
Daily Mirror, 5 July 1948: 9.5D; Evan Davies, *Aspects of Modern World History*, Hodder
and Stoughton, 1990: 5.6C; Isaac Deutscher, *Stalin*, Oxford University Press, 1961:
5.6G; M. N. Duffy, *The Twentieth Century*, Basil Blackwell, 1964: 4.3B; Anne Frank,
The Diary of Anne Frank, Viking, 1989: 7.6C; Government Public Information Leaflet,
July 1939, Imperial War Museum: 8.4A; Government Public Information Leaflet No 4,
July 1939: 8.3B; *The Guardian*, 'The Land Army reunion', January 1984: 8.2F;
Hampshire Chronicle, 11 November 1916: 4.1D; Hampshire Record Office,
Hampshire in the Great War, Hampshire County Council, 1985: 3.8E; Scott and Hilary
Harrison, *Questioning History 5 'The Modern World'*, Macmillan, 1991: 9.1B, 9.1C;
James Hemming, *Mankind against the Killers*, Longman, 1956: 3.9B; C. P. Hill,
Franklin Roosevelt, Oxford University Press, 1966: 7.11E; Maureen Hill, *Growing up at
War*, Armada, 1989: 8.3E; Tony Howarth, *The World Since 1900*, Longman, 1979: 7.5D,
9.3A; M. Jones, *Life in Britain in World War Two*, Batsford, 1983: 8.2E; Nigel Kelly,
The Second World War, Heinemann Educational, 1989: 6.4A; Derek Lambert,
The Sheltered Days, Andre Deutsch, 1965: 8.3D; Basil Liddell Hart, *History of the
Second World War*, Cassell, 1970: 7.2B, 7.9A; P. Mantin and C. Lankester, *From
Romanov to Gorbachev*, Hutchinson, 1989: 5.6D; J. Martell, *The Twentieth-Century
World*, Harrap, 1969: 5.2C; Christopher Martin, *English Life in the First World War*,
Wayland, 1988: 3.7E, 3.7F, 3.8D; Christopher Martin, *War Poems*, Unwin Hyman,
1990: 3.10C; Christopher Martin, *The War Poets*, Wayland, 1983: 3.10G; Howard
Martin, *Britain since 1800: The Welfare State*, Macmillan Education, 1988: 3.8F;
Rupert Martin, *Looking at Italy*, A & C Black, 1966: 5.2F; Trevor May, *An Economic
and Social History of Britain, 1760–1970*, Longman, 1987: 3.3G; D. B. O'Callaghan,

Roosevelt and the United States, Longman, 1966: 7.11B; George Orwell, *Homage to
Catalonia*, Penguin, 1966: 6.3C; H. L. Peacock, *Europe and Beyond*, Heinemann
Educational, 1974: 9.3B; Ed Rayner and Ron Stapley, *World History*, Longman,
1988: 1.3G; Erich Remarque, *All Quiet on the Western Front*, Putnam, 1980: 2.2C;
E. Roberts, *Stalin: Man of Steel*, Methuen, 1968: 5.6F; J. Roberts and A. Lowe, *Making
the Present*, Hutchinson, 1975: 5.7E; John Robottom, *A Social and Economic History
of Industrial Britain*, Longman, 1986: 3.3F; A. L. Rowse, *The Churchills*, Book Club
Associates, 1966: 6.5C; *Sanity*, August 1985: 7.5F; Paul Shuter and Terry Lewis, *Skills
in History 3*, Heinemann Educational, 1988: 7.3A, 7.6D, 7.6E, 7.9D, 9.1D; Peter
Simkins, *Kitchener's Army*, Manchester University Press, 1988: 3.5C, 3.5D, 3.5E, 3.5F,
3.5G; W. O. Simpson, *Changing Horizons: Britain 1914-80*, Stanley Thornes, 1986: 3.8A,
3.8D, 6.3B; Robert Skelton (Ed.), *Poetry of the Thirties*, Penguin, 1964: 6.3E; D. J. Steel
and L. Taylor, *The Steels*, Nelson, 1976: 8.3C; Russell Stone, *The Drift to War*,
Heinemann Educational, 1975: 6.4C; N. Tate, *People and Events in the Modern World*,
Hodder & Stoughton, 1989: 5.2D; A. J. P. Taylor, *English History 1914–45*, Oxford
University Press, 1992: 3.4D, 7.9F; A. J. P. Taylor (Ed.), *History of the 20th century*,
Purnell/BPC Publishing, 1973: 1.2B, 2.3E; A. J. P. Taylor, *The Second World War*,
Athlone Press, 1974: 7.8C; A. J. P. Taylor, *The Struggle for Mastery in Euorpe*, Oxford
University Press, 1954: 1.3A; David Thomson, *Europe since Napoleon*, Pelican, 1966:
7.1A, 7.4C, 7.7B; Malcolm Thomson, *The Life and Times of Winston Churchill*,
Odhams, 1946: 6.5B; *The Times*, quoted in *Voices and Images of the Great War
1914–18*, Lyn Macdonald, Penguin, 1991: 3.6A; H. R. Trevor-Roper (Ed.), *The Goebbels
Diaries*, Secker & Warburg, 1978: 7.8E; H. R. Trevor-Roper (Ed.), *Hitler's War
Directives, 1939–45*, Sidgwick & Jackson, 1964: 7.3A; *Up The Line to Death – The War
Poets 1914–18*. Anthology selected by Brian Gardner, Eyre Methuen, 1978: 3.10A,
3.10B; *UN General Assembly Official Records*. In Peter Mantin, *Questions of
Evidence – the 20th Century World*, Hutchinson, 1987: 9.2D; *US Department of State
Bulletin*. In Peter Mantin, *Questions of Evidence – the 20th Century World*,
Hutchinson, 1987: 9.2A; Alan White and Eric Hadley, *Germany 1918–1949*, Collins,
1990: 5.5D; John Wroughton and Denys Cook (Eds.), *Documents on World History*,
Macmillan, 1976: 9.4B